Sugar 'n Spice
& OTHER THINGS NICE...

Lorraine Stangness

and

Patt Evans

Published by

Country Creations

Box 742, Strathmore, Alberta
Canada T0J 3H0

PRINTED IN CANADA

Acknowledgments

From Right to Left,
Back: Bruce Webb,
Darlene McCorrister,
Chris Basham,
Melinda Brown,
Gail Ford,
Betty Lawson,
Sandy Wey,
Janet Samuels.
Front:
Cheryl Rosenquist,
Joanne Baird,
Sam Butterwick and
Caryl Yarmchuk

On September 6 & 7, 1992, twelve quilters gave up their Labour Day long weekend to attend a workshop for Sugar 'n Spice. This is actually not all that unusual as quilters will usually drop everything to be able to sew uninterrupted for two days. Even so, Patt and I will be eternally grateful for the enormous contributions the following people have so graciously donated:

Joanne Baird and Caryl Yarmchuk – Quilter's Cabin, Calgary, Alberta

Cheryl Rosenquist and Bruce Webb – Sonora Yard Goods, Sonora, California

Chris Basham and Melinda Brown – Bearly Stitchin', Pasadena, California

Darlene McCorrister – Darlene's Fabrics, Strathmore, Alberta

Sam Butterwick, Gail Ford, Janet Samuels, Betty Lawsen, and Sandy Wey – Calgary, Alberta

Special Thanks

To Joanne and Caryl of Quilter's Cabin, Calgary, Alberta for offering their shop in which to hold the workshop. Their never ending support and understanding are sincerely appreciated.

Also thanks to:

Bretin's Flower Farm, Calgary, Alberta for providing the dried flower arrangements.

Modeling by Karen Planden, Calgary, Alberta and Harry Evans, Indus, Alberta

Photography by Harry Planden – Calgary, Alberta

Graphics and Layout by Wallymolly Works – Calgary, Alberta

Printing by Unicom Graphics Ltd.– Calgary, Alberta

ISBN: 0-9696388-0-9

First Printing, 1992.

SIDE QUILTING TEMPLATE FOR CIRCLE OF LOVE – SEE PAGE 26

QUILTING TEMPLATE FOR KITTY-LICIOUS & ROWS 'N BOWS – SEE PAGES 17 & 20

CORNER QUILTING TEMPLATE FOR CIRCLE OF LOVE – SEE PAGE 26

Cut this
Template page
from book for use.

Cut this
Template page
from book for use.

Dedications

I would like to dedicate this book to my
Mom and Scotty.
To my Mom for all the loving attention and
understanding she has showered
upon me throughout my entire life and
to Scotty for the love and companionship he has given
my mother and all of us within our family.

Lorraine

This book is dedicated
to my husband
Russ
for his love, support and encouragement;
to my son
Harry
for inspiration and to my
Grandma Molly
for sharing her love of quilting.

Patt

Lorraine Stangness

"There's never enough time!" Now here's a phrase well known to most quiltmakers and Lorraine Stangness is no exception. Holding down a full time bookkeeping job, teaching classes and seminars, managing her pattern company, Country Creations, as well as spending time with her husband and four sons, keeps Lorraine on the go!

Piecework and quiltmaking create a release for Lorraine's designing abilities and the stimulus that spurs her on to further discoveries. Sharing this ability and knowledge with the students in her classes and seminars and hopefully creating within them an excitement about the craft she so loves has been a longtime goal for Lorraine.

The success of her first book "Heaven's Above", Boyd Publishing, in which she first introduced the unique concept of grid sections for pictorial quilts, was a surprise as well as a delight for Lorraine.

Lorraine lives with her husband, Gordon, on a farm near Strathmore, Alberta. Gordon is very involved with Lorraine in all aspects of her business and also lends the support required for her to maintain her busy schedule. Shawn and Tyler live with them on the farm. Greg and his wife Anita, live in Airdrie and Brad lives near them in Calgary.

Patt Evans

Patt has long appreciated the art of quiltmaking. She is not a quiltmaker herself but her exposure to this art form has been life-long. Her grandma's quilts have been a part of her parents and her own home.

An artist and a designer, Patt's inspiration for these quilt designs came after the birth of her first child, Harry. The presence of a child in her life, and her working relationship with Lorraine helped her create these quilt designs for the "young at heart".

Lorraine's interpretation of Patt's designs have been an exciting and rewarding process.

Patt and her husband, Russ, both work from their home at Indus, Alberta, a small hamlet outside the city of Calgary. She is busy juggling a full-time graphics business, Wallymolly Works, a very young child and helping her husband in his work.

Sugar 'n Spice
& OTHER THINGS NICE...
Table of Contents

Introduction

Sugar 'n Spice & Other Things Nice is a special quilt instruction book containing several unique designs that will stimulate excitement in the very young and also in the "young at heart".

Dolls, Dinosaurs and Kittens are easily pieced and set into numerous quilt and quilted project designs. The designs in the book are all based on an innovative new concept of a "grid system". Any and all of the designs can be sewn using a grid size determined by the sewer. Whether you are a miniature quilt specialist or a bed size quilt lover, this "grid system" will work for you.

Section One of the book takes you through the quiltmaking process from beginning to end. You will find suggestions on "tools of the trade", cutting strips and fabric choices right through to the final step of binding the project. These suggestions should be helpful as you progress through the stages of quilt construction.

Sugar 'n Spice, Section Two, consists of detailed charts, diagrams and instructions for the completion of several unique designs that can vary from small wall hangings to large bed quilts depending on which "grid size" is chosen. Fabric requirements and instructions are given for one particular grid size but these are easily adaptable to any of the six grid sizes on the conversion chart.

Section Three, Other Things Nice, is a collection of wonderful accessories to either coordinate with quilts from Section Two or to make as individual projects. Bibs, Pillows, Soft Sculpture and a marvellous new tote bag produce the stimulus that make the "creative juices" being to flow within us.

The Five "E's", which is the last section, is intended to uncover the creative abilities within us all and to stimulate these abilities with a few suggestions to help along the way.

Quilting, to me, is an art form within which I am able to express with fabric my innermost feelings interpreted through the designs of the projects. It is my relaxation, stimulus, and companion as well as the outlet for any creative abilities that I may have. The original designs in this book, by Patt Evans, have inspired within me the creation of the actual projects and we both hope they will give you as much pleasure and satisfaction as we have experienced during the process of completing "Sugar 'n Spice".

The Grids

A. How They Work

The grid system utilized in this book is an innovative new concept that will dazzle your imagination! One single design can be made into a miniature quilt or a full size bed quilt simply by changing the finished grid size that you use for the construction of the project.

Each project has it's own set of fabric requirements and instructions and will refer to the specific grid diagram and piecing chart required. Each grid diagram can be used in more than one project and suggestions for these numerous variations can be found throughout the book.

The number one rule to remember when reading the grid diagrams is that the numbers printed below each component piece refers to the <u>number of grids and **NOT** measurements.</u> This is where the uniqueness of the system comes in! The same diagram can be used for sewing a 1/4" finished grid or for a 1 1/2" finished grid or for any size in between. They are also easily adapted to the metric system which is boon to those who sew and quilt using that system. The versatility of these grid diagrams is infinite!

Here's how they work...

1. Each grid diagram is broken down into sections, units or rows for ease of cutting, piecing, and assembling.

2. Each section, unit or row is shown as a whole and then shown with each component piece separate (cutting diagram).

3. All of the individual pieces of the grid diagrams and cutting charts have the various fabrics noted on them by the use of symbols, textures or shading to indicate the placement of specific fabrics.

4. The shapes used in all of the grid diagrams are either squares or rectangles. These are simple to cut. Refer to the sizes on the Grid Conversion Chart, Page 9, to determine the correct measurement for the specific pieces.

   eg. A quilt project is being constructed using a 3/4" finished grid. The piece that you are about to cut has the numbers 6 x 8 printed below it. This means that piece is 6 grids wide by 8 grids long. Refer to the Grid Conversion Chart under the finished grid size for 3/4". The piece will be cut 5" x 6 1/2"

When beginning a specific section, unit or row, look over the cutting diagram carefully.

Get an idea of the sizes that need to be cut from a certain fabric. If there are a number of pieces that are 6 grids wide, for example, then cut a whole strip to that measurement rather than cutting individual pieces. From this cut strip most of the pieces required can be subcut.

5. Many of the squares and rectangles on the grid diagrams are further divided by triangles on the corners. These are called connector corners. I learned this very fascinating technique from Mary Ellen Hopkins, a pioneer in this concept. The system works so well that you will be amazed and wonder why you ever did it any other way.

6. Some of the triangles are small and some of them are large. Some cover the whole corner of the square or rectangle and others do not. All of the corner triangles start out as cut squares and are applied as shown in further instructions. Study the examples in the diagrams below in order to understand the method used to determine the size to cut the squares for the corner triangles.

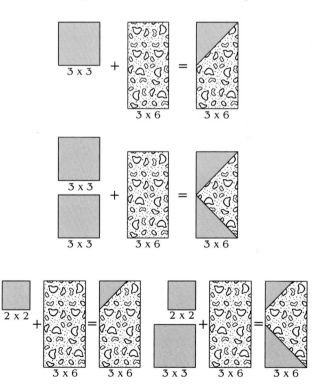

Most of the sizes required for the corner square are fairly obvious but if they are not, use the see-thru grid provided at the back of the book. Lay this over the pieces on the diagrams so that you can determine the grid size of the corner squares.

7. I recommend using a piece of thermolam or flannel approximately 24" x 36" to place the pieces for the sections as they are cut. The pieces will cling to the thermolam to prevent your arrangements from moving as you work. They may also be taken from your cutting area and placed above or beside your sewing machine for accessibility.

8. Follow the steps listed below for each section, unit or row:

   a) Study the diagram, decide on fabric placement and then cut tiny pieces of each fabric and tack them to the corresponding symbol on the cutting diagram. This will keep you from getting mixed up as to which fabric goes where.

   b) Refer to the Grid Conversion Chart, Page 9, for the correct sizes to cut the pieces for the finished grid size you have chosen.

   c) Cut all the pieces for the specific cutting diagram you are working on and arrange the pieces on the thermolam to look like those on the cutting diagram. Place the corner squares at an angle to the pieces they will be sewn to. See Diagram #1.

Dino-Mite! SECTION 1 – Diagram #1

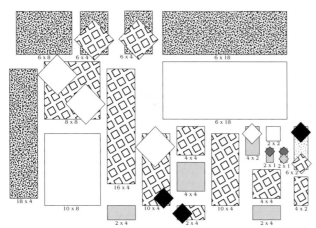

9. Sewing the Sections

   Take your laid out section to your sewing area and place it in a strategic location.

   a) Sewing the Corner Squares

   – place a corner square RIGHT SIDES TOGETHER and raw edges even with the piece it will be sewn to.

   – stitch across the diagonal of the corner square through both layers.

   – trim the seam allowance of the TOP SQUARE ONLY to 1/4".

   – press the remaining top triangle over the cut seam allowance.

   – the uncut bottom piece will be the stitching guide when joining to other pieces; therefore, any shortage of the cut

triangles will be within the seam allowance. See Diagram #2.

Diagram #2

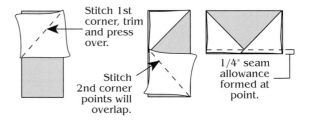

Stitch on diagonal line.

Trim seam allowance to 1/4" on the Top Corner fabric ONLY.

Use base piece as seam guide.

   – when a piece has two corner squares that will intersect, apply the corner square one at a time as shown in the following diagram.

Diagram #3

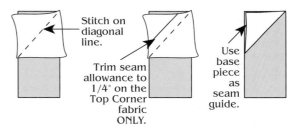

Stitch 1st corner, trim and press over.

Stitch 2nd corner points will overlap.

1/4" seam allowance formed at point.

   b) When all of the corner triangles are sewn in place, return the pieces to their correct positions on the thermolam.

   c) Groupings of small pieces should be sewn together before they are sewn to the larger pieces. These are then sewn into rows and finally the rows are sewn together to form the completed section.

   d) The pieces themselves will usually dictate which way to press. Pressing towards the darker fabric will not always apply when sewing these sections, units and rows. In some instances, though, to ensure having seam allowances of connecting rows pressed in opposite directions, you may want to press the seam allowance against the way it wants to go.

10. You have now completed one section, unit or row. This is the part of this whole system that excites me the most. You can cut, assemble and sew one section at a time, place that sewn section on your design wall, stand back and be absolutely thrilled with what you've created. It is a completed portion of the project as a whole and acts as the stimulus to begin on another section to see how it will look. Before long, and without realizing it, the sections are all sewn and ready to sew together into the whole project!

Grid Conversion Chart

FINISHED GRID SIZE GRID #	1/4"	1/2"	3/4"	1"	1 1/4"	1 1/2"
1/2	5/8"	3/4"	7/8"	1"	1 1/8"	1 1/4"
1	3/4"	1"	1 1/4"	1 1/2"	1 3/4"	2"
1 1/2	7/8"	1 1/4"	1 5/8"	2"	2 3/8"	2 3/4"
2	1"	1 1/2"	2"	2 1/2"	3"	3 1/2"
2 1/2	1 1/8"	1 3/4"	2 3/8"	3"	3 5/8"	4 1/4"
3	1 1/4"	2"	2 3/4"	3 1/2"	4 1/4"	5"
4	1 1/2"	2 1/2"	3 1/2"	4 1/2"	5 1/2"	6 1/2"
5	1 3/4"	3"	4 1/4"	5 1/2"	6 3/4"	8"
6	2"	3 1/2"	5"	6 1/2"	8"	9 1/2"
7	2 1/4"	4"	5 3/4"	7 1/2"	9 1/4"	11"
8	2 1/2"	4 1/2"	6 1/2"	8 1/2"	10 1/2"	12 1/2"
9	2 3/4"	5"	7 1/4"	9 1/2"	11 3/4"	14"
10	3"	5 1/2"	8"	10 1/2"	13"	15 1/2"
11	3 1/4"	6"	8 3/4"	11 1/2"	14 1/4"	17"
12	3 1/2"	6 1/2"	9 1/2"	12 1/2"	15 1/2"	18 1/2"
13	3 3/4"	7"	10 1/4"	13 1/2"	16 3/4"	20"
14	4"	7 1/2"	11"	14 1/2"	18"	21 1/2"
15	4 1/4"	8"	11 3/4"	15 1/2"	19 1/4"	23"
16	4 1/2"	8 1/2"	12 1/2"	16 1/2"	20 1/2"	24 1/2"
17	4 3/4"	9"	13 1/4"	17 1/2"	21 3/4"	26"
18	5"	9 1/2"	14"	18 1/2"	23"	27 1/2"
19	5 1/4"	10"	14 3/4"	19 1/2"	24 1/4"	29"
20	5 1/2"	10 1/2"	15 1/2"	20 1/2"	25 1/2"	30 1/2"
21	5 3/4"	11"	16 1/4"	21 1/2"	26 3/4"	32"
22	6"	11 1/2"	17"	22 1/2"	28"	33 1/2"
23	6 1/4"	12"	17 3/4"	23 1/2"	29 1/4"	35"
24	6 1/2"	12 1/2"	18 1/2"	24 1/2"	30 1/2"	36 1/2"
25	6 3/4"	13"	19 1/4"	25 1/2"	31 3/4"	38"
26	7"	13 1/2"	20"	26 1/2"	33"	39 1/2"
27	7 1/4"	14"	20 3/4"	27 1/2"	34 1/4"	41"
28	7 1/2"	14 1/2"	21 1/2"	28 1/2"	35 1/2"	42 1/2"
29	7 3/4"	15"	22 1/4"	29 1/2"	36 3/4"	44"
30	8"	15 1/2"	23"	30 1/2"	38"	45 1/2"
31	8 1/4"	16"	23 3/4"	31 1/2"	39 1/4"	46"
32	8 1/2"	16 1/2"	24 1/2"	32 1/2"	40 1/2"	47 1/2"
33	8 3/4"	17"	25 1/4"	33 1/2"	41 3/4"	49"
34	9"	17 1/2"	26"	34 1/2"	43"	50 1/2"
35	9 1/4"	18"	26 3/4"	35 1/2"	44 1/4"	51"
36	9 1/2"	18 1/2"	27 1/2"	36 1/2"	45 1/2"	52 1/2"

SECTION ONE: General Instructions

A. Basic Equipment and Supplies

There are many tools and sewing aids on the market today that make quiltmaking much easier and faster than ever before. These things are very important, but of greater importance is the condition of them. Make sure you regularly clean and oil your sewing machine, change the needles often, keep your scissors sharpened and make sure your rotary cutter is free from nicks. Having your equipment in good working order will make your sewing much more pleasurable. Below find a list of suggested quiltmaking equipment:

    Sewing Machine – in good working order
    Extra Machine Needles
    Self-healing cutting mat
    Rotary Cutter
    Template Ruler – 6" wide – both 12" and
                                      24" lengths
    Small Scissors
    Fabric Marker – test before using

B. Important Terms

Listed below are some of the terms and definitions referred to throughout the instructions of this book.

1. **1/4" Seam Allowance** – All of the seam allowances in this book refer to a SCANT 1/4". Practice on some scrap pieces of fabric. Cut two pieces of fabric 3 1/2" x 2". Stitch the 3 1/2" side of the two pieces right sides together with a SCANT 1/4" seam allowance. Press the seam allowance in one direction. Measure the sewn piece – it should measure EXACTLY 3 1/2" x 3 1/2". If it does not, you must adjust your seam allowance accordingly.

2. **Grain Lines and Cutting Strips** – There are two straight grain lines on woven fabric. The lengthwise grain runs parallel to the selvages and has very little give to it. The crosswise grain runs perpendicular to the selvage edges and has much more give to it. "Cutting a Strip" refers to cutting on the crossgrain of the fabric from selvage to selvage.

3. **Cut Size** – This refers to the size that the strip or piece of fabric is cut BEFORE stitching. The grids shown on the piecing diagrams throughout the book are the cut size. You must choose the grid size and refer to the Grid Conversion Chart for the actual cutting size.

4. **Finished Size** – This refers to the size of a piece of fabric after it is sewn into the quilt top with a SCANT 1/4" seam allowance.

C. Fabric Choices

1. Fabric Content

It has been my experience that using 100% cotton fabric makes the piecing procedure for completing a quilt top much easier and less frustrating than using poly blends. I highly recommend a trip to your local quilt shop where you will find the best variety of high quality cottons and the expertise from the staff that is such an asset when selecting fabrics for a quilt.

2. Fabric Selection

The first decision to be made, of course, is to determine the intended purpose of the quilt or quilted project. Is the project for a baby, a teenager or a good friend who is "young at heart"? Will it be a wall hanging that will coordinate with a specific room's decor? Will it be a "cuddle" quilt that will be well used? Will the recipient prefer (or require) dark colours, bright colours, pastels and soft warm colours or high contrast colours?

For the designs in this book, it is very important to have high contrast between the background fabric and the fabrics used to create the design. I would recommend choosing the background fabric first and then choosing the fabrics that will work the best with it for the designs.

Try to use a variety of prints and solids in your fabric selection. The use of large and small prints, stripes, dots or plains will add visual appeal to your quilt. Texture variation in the fabrics of the project will add interest.

3. Tips for Specific Designs

The following suggestions are founded on experiences I encountered while completing some of the projects in the book. While working on the designs I learned many lessons on which fabrics worked well and which did not. I have a couple of quilt tops to keep as reminders to my students and to myself attesting to these failures. I hope you will find the suggestions below helpful as you make your fabric selections.

a) Kitten Projects

   – if the kittens are to be a variety of colours, make sure that they are very different from each other. Putting a green kitten beside a blue kitten of the same value will not work well as the two will tend to blend.

- the kittens may be made from one colour family but they must be very different in value. **eg.** very light blue, medium blue, very dark blue.
- the bows on the kittens need to have a high contrast to the kitten fabric and the background fabric.
- the eyes and nose, like the bows, also require high contrast.
- choose background fabric carefully. Subtle prints with all over texture will create movement in the quilt.

b. **Dinosaur Projects**
- again, high contrast is required between the background fabric and the fabrics used in the designs.
- the background fabric may be a fairly busy print as long as the fabrics used in the designs are strong enough to dominate the background print.

c. **Doll Projects**
- the faces, arms and legs of the dolls should not be too light in colour such as a white or a very pale pink. The very light fabrics tends to take over the design rather than blend.
- as with the previous designs, high contrast is required between the background fabric and fabrics for the dolls. A large print does not seem to work very well as a background fabric as the delicate doll design loses itself within an overwhelming background. Subtle, delicate background fabrics or very small two colour prints seem to be the most suitable.
- the bow and accent fabric should be very different in value from the hair and the dress to keep the fabrics from blending. A distinction between these fabrics is essential to the definition of the design.

D. Fabric Preparation

1. **To Wash or Not to Wash** – that is the question! If you are using a top quality 100% cotton fabric it is not necessary to pre-wash the fabric but it is necessary to test the fabrics for colour fastness. Cut a small piece of the fabrics that you are unsure of. Place each of them one at a time in a bowl of hot water with a piece of white cotton. Let sit for a couple of hours. Remove the fabrics and rinse the white fabric. The water may show some colour from the test fabric but as long as that colour has not **transferred** to the white cotton, it is safe to use. Not pre-washing, of course, is a personal choice.

2. **Straighten and Fold the Fabric** – Fold the fabric in half, selvage to selvage and wrong sides together. Make sure the selvages are lined up. If they do not, you may have to pull on the fabric corner to corner (on the bias) and refold the fabric. Repeat this process until the selvages line up. When they are lined up bring the fold of the fabric up again to meet the selvage edge. You will now have 4 layers of fabric.

3. **Squaring Up and Cutting Strips** – The instructions given below are for a right handed person. If you are left handed, do exactly the opposite.

   a) Place the template ruler along the right hand side of the folded fabric. Line up a horizontal line on the ruler along the double fold of the fabric and have the edge of the ruler far enough into the fabric to insure cutting the uneven edges of all 4 layers. Cut along the edge of the ruler with your rotary cutter. You now have a clean, square edge from which to begin measuring.

   b) **NOTE – Square UP & Flip!** Square up the fabric on the right hand edge and then FLIP the fabric end for end so that the squared edge is now on the left hand side and the selvages are still at the top, away from you. See Diagram #4.

Diagram #4

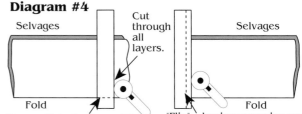

   c) **Measuring** – Lay the desired measurement of the ruler along the squared up side of the fabric. Keep a horizontal line of the ruler along the double fold as well. Cut the strip.

   d) **Subcutting** – The cut strips will have to be subcut into the required lengths of pieces as stated on the Grid Conversion Chart. Remove the selvage edges from the strip. Line up the vertical measurement and a horizontal line on the ruler to the strip and subcut the required size piece.

E. Border Applications

Some of the quilt projects in the book use the Log Cabin Style border and others use the Mitered Style border. Instructions are given for both styles.

1. LOG CABIN STYLE

a) **Measure for the side borders** – Measure the quilt top along one side, in the middle and along the other side. See Diagram #5. These measurements may vary. Take an average of the three measurements and record. Piece, if necessary, to make a strip long enough for this measurement. Cut both side borders to the exact measurement recorded.

Diagram #5

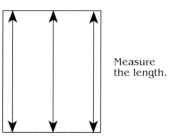

Measure the length.

b) **Apply the side borders** – Find the center of the sides of the quilt top and mark. Find the center of the side border strips and mark. Matching center markings, pin the side borders to the quilt top, slightly easing or stretching to fit.

c) **Measure the top and bottom borders.** Measure the quilt top along the top edge, the middle and the bottom edge. See Diagram #6. Take an average of these three measurements and record. Piece if necessary to make a strip long enough for this measurement. Cut the top and bottom borders to the exact measurement recorded.

Diagram #6

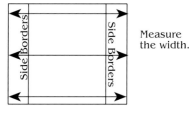

Measure the width.

d) **Apply the Top and Bottom Borders** – Find the center of the top and bottom of the quilt top and mark. Find the center of the top and bottom border strips and mark. Matching center markings, pin the top and bottom borders to the quilt top, slightly easing or stretching to fit.

e) **Applying Additional Borders** – The first border is the most important of the borders as it determines whether or not your quilt will be square. Once it is applied and you are sure that the quilt top is square, the additional borders may be applied without further measuring. Be sure to arrange the seams of the borders so that they are staggered rather than lined up.

2. MITERED STYLE

a) Determine the width of all the borders when they are sewn together. eg. Border #1 is 1" finished, Border #2 is 1 1/2" finished, and Border #3 is 2 1/2" finished. These three borders total 5" finished. Double this measurement and add 4" = 14". Measure the width and length of the quilt top using the same method as measuring for the Log Cabin Style. See Diagram #5. Use these measurements to determine the length required for the border strip sets:

Width of Quilt + 14" = _____
Length of Quilt + 14" = _____

b) **Sewing the Strip Sets** – Once you have joined the strips together to form the required lengths, sew the required border strips for each border together to form a border strip set. You should have four strip sets – two sides and the top and bottom borders. Remember to stagger the seams of each border strip set rather than having them lined up.

c) Find the center of the top and bottom edge of the quilt top and mark. Find the center of the top and bottom border strips and mark. Matching the markings, and right sides together, pin the border strips to the quilt top and bottom. Begin stitching 1/4" from the edge of the quilt and end stitching 1/4" from the other edge of the quilt. Backstitch at both points, being careful not to stitch further than the 1/4" point. See Diagram #8.

Diagram #8

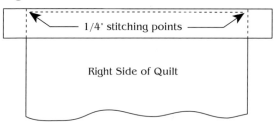

1/4" stitching points

Right Side of Quilt

d) Measure, mark and pin the side borders in the same manner as the top and bottom borders. Now turn the quilt over and stitch the border strip set on from the WRONG SIDE of the quilt top. (The border strip set is pinned, of course, to the right side of the quilt). By doing this you can see EXACTLY where to begin and end stitching – at the same 1/4" point as for the top and bottom borders.

e) **To Miter the Corners** – Fold the quilt top right sides together on the diagonal to one corner. Line up the border strips and pin to hold in place. Draw a 45° angle from the 1/4" stitching point to the raw edge of the border strip. Stitch on this drawn line remembering not to stitch further in than the 1/4" stitching point. See Diagram #9.

Diagram #9

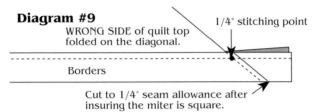

WRONG SIDE of quilt top folded on the diagonal.

1/4" stitching point

Borders

Cut to 1/4" seam allowance after insuring the miter is square.

F. Pre-Quilting Decisions

1. Marking the Quilt Top

a) Most of the quilting on the projects in this book was accomplished by machine. That, of course, is a personal choice. (And a very short deadline). Some of the projects require only "in the ditch" quilting as the design of the project itself is intense enough not to require further embellishment. Others, with more open space, are enhanced wonderfully with some machine or hand quilted designs in those open spaces. Suggestions for quilting designs are referred to in the instructions for some individual projects. Quilting designs, other than "in the ditch", should be marked on the quilt top at this time.

b) There are many types of markers, chalk, soapstone and pencils on the market that will work great for marking the quilt design onto the quilt top. Check with your local quilt shop for suggestions on which of their products they recommend. Before using any product to mark your quilt top, test the marker on scraps of fabric that were used in the quilt top. Mark some designs on the fabric scraps, wash and dry the scrap and check to see if the marks have disappeared. If they have, it is safe to mark the quilt top.

c) Very dark fabrics require a cardboard or plastic template to trace around onto the quilt top as it is difficult to see through these fabrics on a light table. A light table works well with medium and light coloured fabrics. I use a homemade light table – open your kitchen or dining room table about one foot (or as wide as it will open), place an 18" x 30" piece of glass or plexiglass over the opening, and place a lamp (without the shade) under the opening about 6" from the glass – you have created

your very own light table. Proceed to trace the design onto your quilt top.

2. Choosing the Batting

Choosing the batting is a personal choice as well as a decision based on the purpose of the project whether it be a wall hanging, a bed quilt or another quilted project. The look you wish to achieve and the amount of quilting required to accomplish this are also determining factors in batting choices. Below find the descriptions and characteristics of two types of batting commonly used.

a) **Cotton or Cotton/Polyester Blend Batting**

– will shrink 3 to 4 inches when washed.

– if you complete the quilting and then wash the quilt, you will achieve an antique look to your quilt.

– pre-washing the quilt batting will allow it to shrink before it is put into the quilt and the completed quilt will change very little in appearance after washing.

– quilting at intervals no further apart than 1 1/2" is required on 100% cotton battings.

– cotton/polyester blend battings may be quilted at slightly larger intervals (up to 2" - 2 1/2").

b) **Polyester Bonded Batting**

– does not shrink when washed therefore does not require pre-washing.

– finished quilt has a very smooth look.

– many thicknesses to choose from and choice will depend on the project.

– quilting can be spaced at 4" - 5" intervals.

Diagram #10

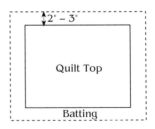

2" – 3"

Quilt Top

Batting

NOTE: The batting should be 2" – 3" larger all around than the quilt top.

G. Machine Quilting

1. Suggested Equipment

a) **Even Feed Foot** – The even feed foot (or "walking foot") is an essential tool for machine quilting. It provides a set of feed dogs on top of the fabric, prevents the

Machine Quilting Continued...

layers from shifting and therefore allows all three layers to move at the same speed when quilting. Ask your sewing machine dealer about the even feed foot best suited for your particular sewing machine.

b) **Needles** – Either a size 10/70 or 12/80 is recommended. Use the best needle you can afford and a new needle for every project.

c) **Thread** – Use 100% cotton thread in the bobbin that will match the backing fabric. For the top of the quilt either 100% cotton thread or transparent nylon thread is suitable. Polyester thread is not recommended as it is too strong and may, in time, cut the fibers of the fabric. Transparent nylon thread is suggested if your quilting progresses over many colours. It is available in clear or smoke. The clear is recommended for quilts with lighter fabrics and the smoke for quilts with darker fabrics. I do not recommend transparent thread if the quilted project is for a baby or toddler. If the stitches loosen, their tiny fingers could get cut on this very strong thread.

d) **Stitch Length** – Eight to ten stitches per inch (or a setting of 3 1/2 to 4) is recommended for machine quilting.

e) **Bicycle Clips** – These come in very handy for larger projects that require rolling to enable them to fit through the arm of the machine. Clip them to the rolled sections to hold the roll in place as you quilt.

2. The Backing

The methods in which quilt backing is sewn together may vary greatly. Conserving fabric, of course, is a primary concern but the placement of seams on a one colour backing is also important. To achieve the fewest seams and also to use the fabric most efficiently, use a horizontal or a vertical seam on the quilt backing. See Diagram #11.

Diagram #11

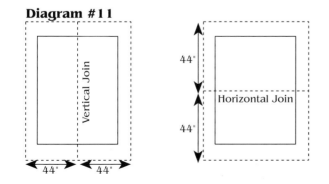

The backing should be 2" – 3" larger than the quilt top all around.

NOTE: Always remove the selvages from both edges of the fabric before stitching together for the quilt backing.

3. Layering – "Making the Sandwich"

When you make a sandwich for lunch, you put a layer of meat, cheese, etc. between two pieces of bread. A quilt sandwich isn't very different – put quilt batting between the quilt top and the backing fabric!

To Make Your Quilt Sandwich:

a) Lay the pressed backing WRONG SIDES UP on a large flat surface.

b) Using one inch pieces of masking tape, secure the backing to the flat surface by placing the tape at intervals of about 10" all around the edges of the backing. Do not stretch the backing but make sure that it is flat.

c) Lay the batting on top of the backing and pat into place. Do not pull on the batting as this may cause the batting to separate in places.

d) Lay the quilt top RIGHT SIDE UP on the batting. Smooth into place, making sure all straight lines and border fabrics stay straight.

e) Pin the quilt through all layers using 1" nickel plated safety pins. Place the pins no further than 3" apart. Begin pinning in the center of the quilt and work out towards the edges until the entire quilt is pinned. Try to avoid pinning on the lines that are to be quilted.

4. Machine Quilting

Machine quilting puts a great deal of strain on your shoulder and neck muscles. All the while I am machine quilting, I have a saying which I repeat to myself. "This quilt would take me six months to complete if I were hand quilting!" I love the exquisite look of a hand quilted project and usually have a least one on the go but for those dozens of new quilt patterns that I just have to try, machine quilting is more expeditious. Great machine quilters such as Harriet Hargrave, have mastered the art of machine quilting to such a degree that one is in awe when witnessing the intricate designs accomplished. I highly recommend Harriet's book 'Heirloom Machine Quilting' for comprehensive information on machine quilting.

Below are two suggestions for making the machine quilting process a little easier:

a) Roll the quilt from both edges towards the center of the quilt. Roll horizontally, vertically or diagonally depending on the placement of the quilting lines. Use bicycle clips to hold the rolled quilt in place. By using this procedure the rolled portion of the quilt fits easily between the presser foot and the main body of the machine. Reroll the quilt as necessary as the quilting progresses.

b) Do not pull on the quilt as you stitch but allow the quilt to be fed through by the even feed foot. Place a hand on either side of the presser foot to guide the stitches and to slightly part the loft in the fabric when stitching in the ditch.

H. Binding

There are many theories about binding and its application. I have chosen to describe the binding method that is my preference. This method uses STRAIGHT CROSSGRAIN STRIPS and DOUBLE FOLD BINDING which when applied forms a true sewn miter on both the front and the back of the quilt. When joining strips together for the binding, it is important to use a bias join. This allows the binding seam to be distributed along the edge of the quilt rather than it being in a "lump".

a) **Bias Join** – lay the ends of two strips RIGHT SIDES TOGETHER at right angles to each other.

   – mark a 45 degree angle from corner to corner and stitch.

   – cut the seam allowance to 1/4" and press to one side. See Diagram #12.

Diagram #12

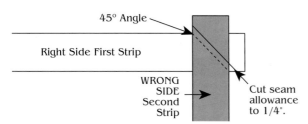

b) **Applying the Binding**

   – measure the length and width of the quilt.

   – join strips together to form 4 bindings:
   Length + 4" (2 sets)
   Width + 4" (2 sets)

   – fold the four binding strips in half lengthwise, WRONG SIDES TOGETHER and press.

– lay a binding strip RIGHT SIDES TOGETHER and raw edges even on the top edge of the quilted project leaving 2" extending past both ends of the quilt.

– backstitch at both points being careful not to go further than the 1/4" point.

– repeat this procedure with the binding on the bottom edge of the quilt. See Diagram #13.

Diagram #13

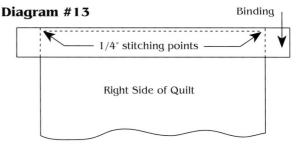

– lay a binding strip RIGHT SIDES TOGETHER and raw edges even on one side of the quilt. Leave 2" extending past the edge on both ends.

– turn the quilt over and stitch the binding on from the WRONG SIDE of the quilt. By doing this, you can see EXACTLY where to begin and end stitching – at the same 1/4" point as for the top and bottom binding.

– after all four bindings are applied, fold the quilt RIGHT SIDES TOGETHER on the diagonal to one corner.

– line up the RIGHT SIDE of the binding strips and pin to hold in place.

– draw a 90 degree angle from the 1/4" stitching point. See Diagram #14.

Diagram #14

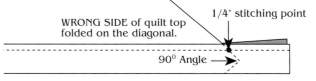

– stitch along the drawn line using very small stitches and matching thread and being careful not to go further into the quilt than the 1/4" stitching point.

– cut the seam allowance to 1/4".

– repeat this procedure for all corners.

– turn the binding to the back of the quilt and pin.

– handstitch the folded edge of the binding in place.

– the corners are mitered on the front and back of the quilt.

SECTION TWO: Sugar 'n Spice

Kitty–Licious!
Quilt

To stitch this quilt called Kitty-Licious
May cause you to become suspicious,

It looks too hard to bother with
But that is just a silly myth,

Follow the charts and sew really straight
The pieces, the layout will begin to relate,

Two rows of kittens with bright coloured ties
Nearing completion the excitement will rise,

You're finished, it's over and Oh! what a lift
To see the delight for this wonderful gift.

Kitty-Licious

This delightful quilt will thrill your young recipient! Colour plates of this quilt are shown on Page 31. The directions and fabric requirements given below are for a 1" finished grid. Find below a list of grid sizes and corresponding quilt sizes if you desire a size different than given in the directions:

1/4"	Finished Grid =	25" x 34"
1/2"	Finished Grid =	35" x 48"
3/4"	Finished Grid =	45" x 62"
1"	**Finished Grid =**	**55" x 76"**
1 1/4"	Finished Grid =	65" x 90"
1 1/2"	Finished Grid =	75" x 104"

Grid Size: 1" Finished Grid

Quilt Size: 55" x 76" Including Borders

Fabric Requirements:

- 1 1/4 yd. (1.2 m) for Kitten, Center Panel and Borders
- 1 1/4 yd. (1.2 m) for Kitten, Center Panel and Borders
- 1 1/4 yd. (1.2 m) for Kitten, Center Panel and Borders
- 2 7/8 yd. (2.6 m) for Background
- 2 1/2" x 30" each of 3 fabrics for Ties
- 2 1/2" x 6" each of 3 fabrics for Tie Knots
- 1 piece 2 1/2" x 18" for Eyes
- 1/3 yd. (.35 m) for Nose and Legs
- 3 1/2 yd. (3.2 m) of Backing Fabric
- 3 1/2 yd. (3.2 m) of Batting
- 5/8 yd. (.6 m) of Binding Fabric

Instructions:

1. Piece two sets of cats following the General Instructions and using the cutting and piecing diagram on Page 19. Refer to the Grid Conversion Chart on Page 9 for the correct sizes to cut for the 1" finished grid.

2. **Center Panel** – cut the following strips 1 1/2" wide:

Background Fabric	–	2 strips
Kitten #1 Fabric	–	1 strip
Kitten #2 Fabric	–	1 strip
Kitten #3 Fabric	–	1 strip

   Sew these strips together to form a strip set. See Diagram #16.

Diagram #16

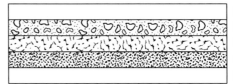

Background
Kitten Fabric #1
Kitten Fabric #2
Kitten Fabric #3
Background

- Measure the width of the kitten panel and cut your strip set to that measurement.
- Pin the center panel to the bottom edge of one kitten panel and to the top edge of the second kitten panel, stitch and press.

3. **First Border** (Background)

   - cut 6 strips of background fabric 3 1/2" wide
   - cut 2 of these strips in half (4 - 22" pieces)
   - stitch one long strip to one half strip – 4 times
   - Measure the length of the quilt body as shown on Page 13. Cut 2 of the sewn border pieces to this measurement. Pin to the sides of the quilt body, matching centers. Stitch and press seam allowances towards the border.
   - Measure the width of the quilt with the side borders as shown on Page 13. Cut the remaining 2 sewn border pieces to this measurement. Pin to the top and bottom of the quilt, matching centers. Stitch and press seam allowances towards the border.

4. **Outside Borders** (3 Kitten Fabrics)

   - cut 7 strips, 2" wide from each of the three kitten fabrics.
   - each round of border will be applied by stitching to the sides first, pressing and then stitching to the top and bottom.
   - sew the following combinations for each of the 3 border fabrics:

Side #1	– 2 long strips
Side #2	– 2 long strips
Top	– 1 long strip + 1/2 strip
Bottom	– 1 long strip + 1/2 strip

5. **Backing** – cut the backing into two equal length pieces. Remove the selvages and stitch the long sides of the two pieces together. Press the seam allowance.

Kitty–Licious!

REMINDER: Sizes refer to number of grids, **NOT** measurements.
See Grid Conversion Chart, Page 9.

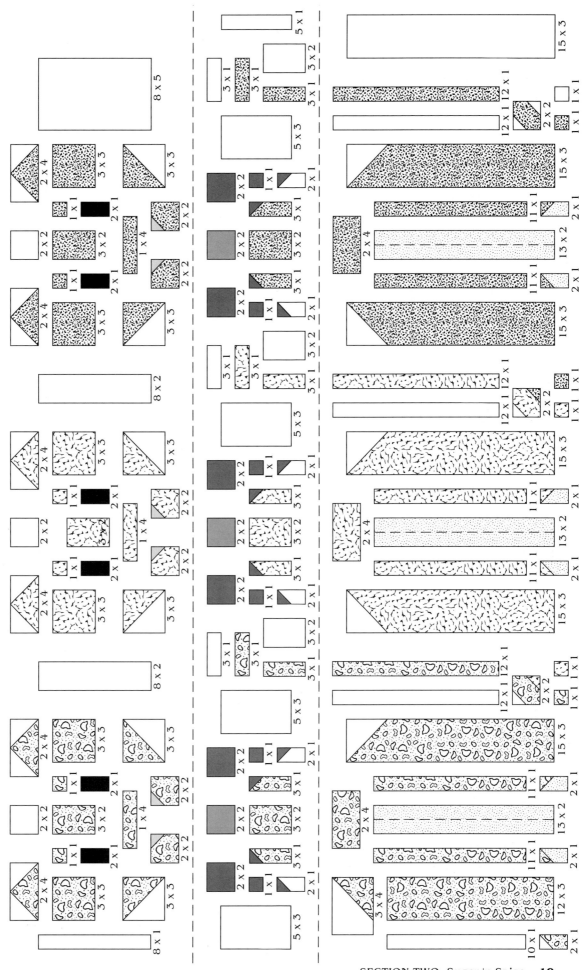

6. **Marking** – See the templates at the front of the book for the pattern for paw-prints if you wish to trace onto the quilt.

7. **Sandwich** – prepare the quilt for quilting as shown on Page 15.

8. **Quilting** – Machine or hand quilt as desired.

9. **Binding** – cut 7 strips of binding fabric 2 1/2" wide. Join pieces as needed following the directions on Page 16. Apply the binding as shown on Page 16.

Rows 'n Bows
WALL HANGING

The kittens sit so straight and tall
To decorate the bedroom wall,

Around their necks are ties so tiny
Add lamé and make them shiny,

The border ties of colours bright
Are very pleasing to the sight,

For young and old this quilt will be
A special gift to you from me!

Colour plates of this wall hanging are shown on Page 30. The instructions and fabric requirements given are for a 1/2" finished grid. Find below a list of grid sizes and corresponding project sizes if you desire a wall hanging size different than given in the instructions:

1/4"	Finished Grid =	16" x 13"
1/2"	**Finished Grid =**	**32" x 26"**
3/4"	Finished Grid =	48" x 39"
1"	Finished Grid =	64" x 52"

Grid Size: 1/2" Finished Grid

Quilt Size: 32" x 26"

Rows 'n Bows

Fabric Requirements:

- 1/4 yd. (.25 m) for Kitten and Border Ties
- 1/4 yd. (.25 m) for Kitten and Border Ties
- 1/4 yd. (.25 m) for Kitten and Border Ties
- 3/4 yd. (.7 m) for Background
- 1 strip 1 1/2" wide for Ties
- 1 piece 1 1/2" x 6" for Tie Knots
- 1 piece 1" x 10" for Eyes
- 1 strip 1 1/2" wide for Nose and Legs
- 1 1/2" x 16" piece for Border Tie Knots
- 1 1/2" x 16" piece for Border Tie Knots
- 1 1/2" x 16" piece for Border Tie Knots
  - 1 piece – 28" x 34" of Backing
  - 1 piece – 28" x 34" of Batting
  - 3/8 yd. (.35 m) of Binding

The instructions below refer to the completion of the inside wall hanging and borders using the 1/2" finished grid size. If you choose another finished grid size for the inside of the wall hanging, continue with that grid size for piecing the bows in the border. **Piece the Bows** for the borders first and measure them **before** cutting and sewing the first plain background borders. The cut width of the plain background borders will depend on the length of the rows of bows. Cut the outside border to the same size as the first background border or to a size of your choice.

Instructions:

1. Piece the 3 kitten panel following the General Instructions and using the cutting and piecing diagram on Page 19. Refer to the Grid Conversion Chart on Page 9 for the correct sizes to cut for the 1/2" finished grid.

2. **First Border** (Background Fabric)
   - cut 2 strips of background fabric 2 1/2" wide.
   - follow the instructions on Page 13 for applying the first border – log cabin style.

3. **Pieced Border**
   - cut 2 strips 1 1/2" wide from each of the three border tie fabrics.

- subcut these strips into 20 - 1 1/2" x 2 1/2" pieces for each fabric.
- subcut each of the 1 1/2" x 16" pieces of border tie knot fabrics into 10 – 1 1/2" x 1 1/2" squares.
- cut 3 strips of background fabric 1 1/2" wide
- subcut these strips into 84 – 1 1/2" squares.
- follow the diagram below and make the following:
  Border Tie #1   –   10
  Border Tie #2   –   9
  Border Tie #3   –   9

Diagram #18

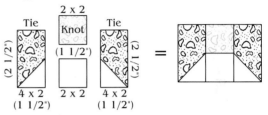

- cut 4 pieces of background fabric 2 1/2" x 2 1/2" for the 4 corners of the pieced border.
- lay out the border ties around the 1st border before stitching in order to alternate the ties in sequential order.
- Side Borders – 6 ties
  Top and Bottom Borders – 8 ties with a 2 1/2" square at each end.
- apply the pieced border in the log cabin style.

4. **Third Border** (Background Fabric)
   - cut 3 strips of background fabric 2 1/2" wide.
   - apply the Third Border in the log cabin style.

5. **Backing** – make sure the backing measures 34" x 28" (2" larger than the wallhanging top).

6. **Marking** – if you wish to do quilting other than "in the ditch", mark the quilt top at this time. Refer to Page 14.

7. **Sandwich** – prepare the quilt for quilting as shown on Page 15.

8. **Quilting** – Machine or hand quilt as desired.

9. **Binding** – cut 4 strips of binding fabric 2 1/2" wide. Apply the binding as shown on Page 16.

Navajo Friendship
QUILT

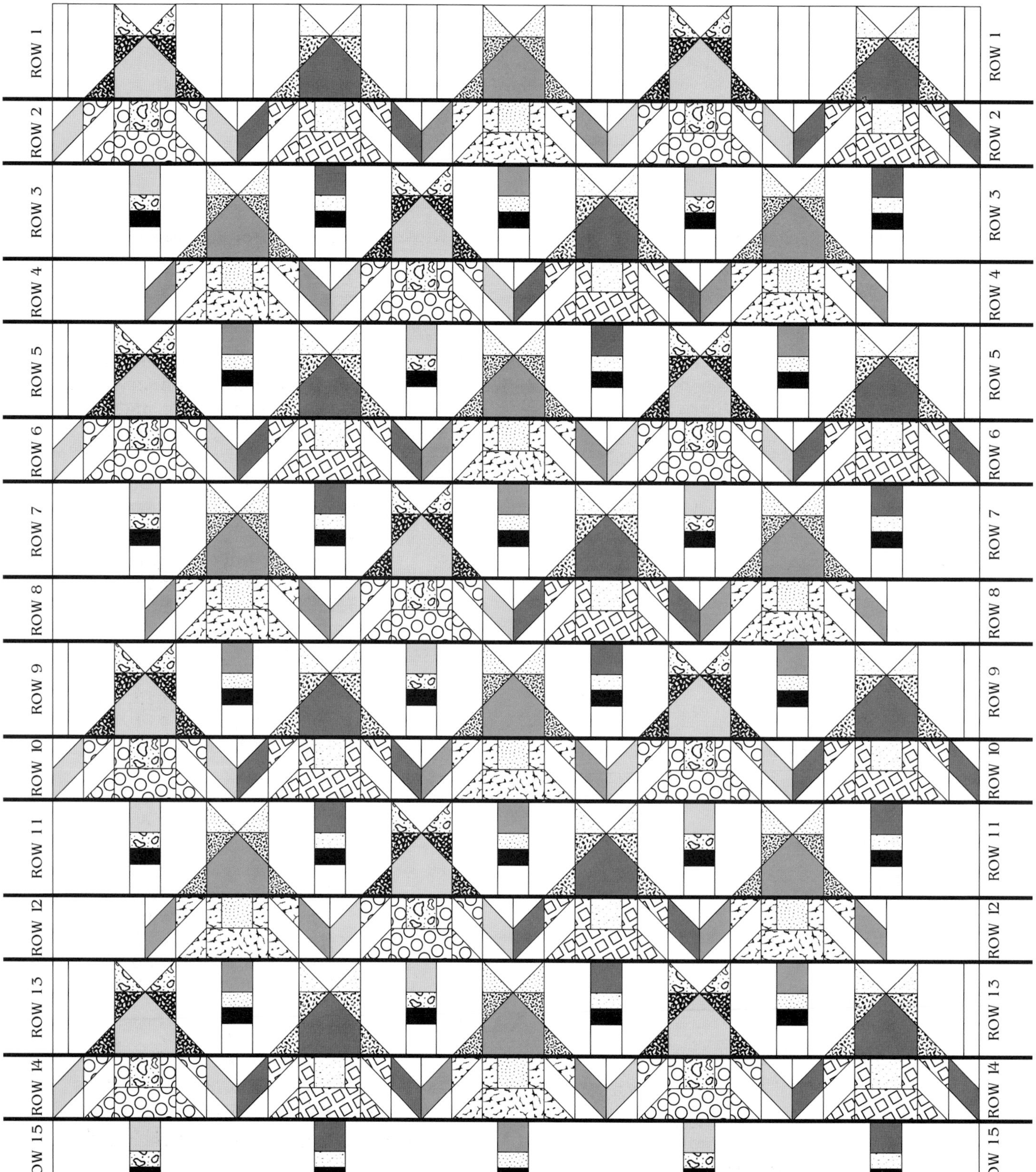

45" x 55 1/2"

Navajo Friendship

Across the vast desert the mountains arise
The sun shines down brightly at early sunrise,

Adobes and palm trees abound on the sand
Providing the shade for the people of the land,

Traditions and customs seem not to end
The importance of life is the love of a friend,

Join hands in a row as these Navajo dolls
And make sure you answer when a friend calls.

The colour plate for 'Navajo Friendship' is shown on Page 35. The instructions and fabric requirements given below are for a 3/4" finished grid. Find below a list of grid sizes and corresponding project sizes if you desire a size different than given in the instructions:

1/4"	Finished Grid =	15" x 18 1/2"
1/2"	Finished Grid =	30" x 37"
3/4"	**Finished Grid =**	**45" x 55 1/2"**
1"	Finished Grid =	60" x 74"
1 1/4"	Finished Grid =	75" x 92 1/2"
1 1/2"	Finished Grid =	90" x 111"

Grid Size: 3/4" Finished Grid

Quilt Size: 54" x 64 1/2" Including Borders

Fabric Requirements:

1/8 yd. (.15 m) Doll #1 – Bow, Socks, Accent

1/8 yd. (.15 m) Doll #1 – Hair

1/4 yd. (.25 m) Doll #1 – Dress

3/8 yd. (.35 m) Doll #1 – Face, Arms, Legs

1/8 yd. (.15 m) Doll #2 – Bow, Socks, Accent

1/8 yd. (.15 m) Doll #2 – Hair

1/4 yd. (.25 m) Doll #2 – Dress

3/8 yd. (.35 m) Doll #2 – Face, Arms, Legs

1/8 yd. (.15 m) Doll #3 – Bow, Socks, Accent

1/8 yd. (.15 m) Doll #3 – Hair

1/4 yd. (.25 m) Doll #3 – Dress

3/8 yd. (.35 m) Doll #3 – Face, Arms, Legs

1/8 yd. (.15 m) for Doll Shoes

2 1/4 yd. (2.0 m) for Background

3/8 yd. (.35 m) for First Border

1 yd. (.9 m) for Second Border

3 5/8 yd. (3.3 m) for Backing

5/8 yd. (.6 m) for Binding

Instructions:

1. There are 21 different units to complete for this quilt. Piece the required number of units following the General Instructions and using the cutting and piecing diagrams on Page 24. Refer to Page 9 for the correct sizes to cut for the 3/4" finished grid.

2. After completing all of the units, sew them together in rows as follows:

NOTE: Follow the full quilt diagram on Page 22 for placement of the units.

Row 1 – 2 unit #1, 2 unit #2, 1 unit #3, 2 unit #13, 2 unit #14, 1 unit #15, 2 unit #10, 2 unit #11, 1 unit #12, 4 unit #17 and 2 unit #16

Row 2, 6, 10 & 14 – 2 unit #4, 2 unit #5 and 1 unit #6

Row 3, 7, 11 – 1 unit #1, 1 unit #2, 2 units #3, 1 unit #13, 1 unit #14, 2 unit #15, 1 unit #10, 1 unit #11, 2 unit #12, 2 unit #7B, 2 unit #8B, 1 unit #9B and 2 unit #18

Row 4, 8, 12 – 1 unit 4, 1 unit #5, 2 unit #6 and 2 unit #19

Row 5, 9, 13 – 2 unit #1, 2 unit #2, 1 unit #3, 1 unit #7B,

(Rows 5, 9 & 13 continued on Page 25)

Navajo Friendship Quilt

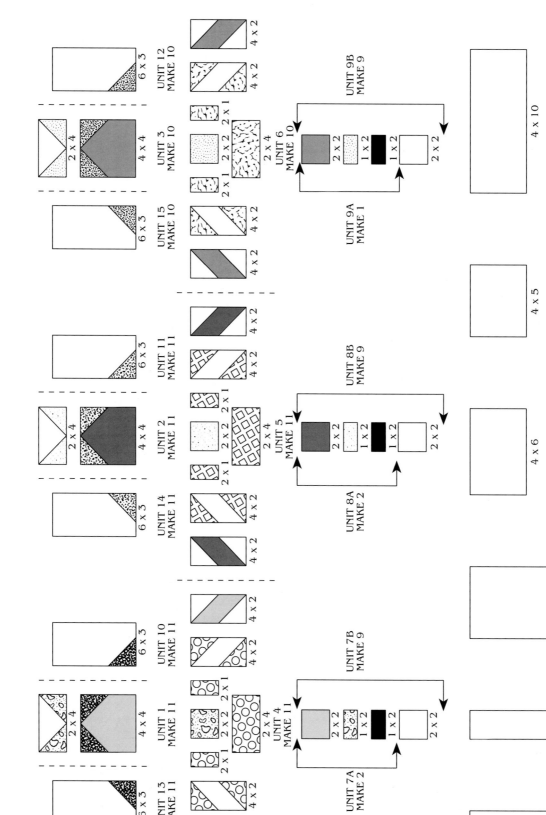

Continued from Page 23...

Navajo Friendship

Row 5, 9,13 – 1 unit #8B, 2 unit #9B,
2 unit #13, 2 unit #14,
1 unit #15, 2 unit #10,
2 unit #11, 1 unit #12 and
2 unit #16

Row 15 – 2 unit #7A, 2 unit #8A,
1 unit #9A, 4 unit #21 and
2 unit #20

3. **First Border** (1" finished)

 – cut 6 strips of first border fabric 1 1/2" wide.

 – cut 2 strips in half.

 – sew 1 long strip to 1 short strip for each border.

 – apply borders using the Log Cabin method as shown on Page 13.

4. **Second Border** (3 1/2" finished)

 – cut 8 strips of second border fabric 4" wide.

 – sew 2 long strips together for each border.

 – apply borders using the Mitered Method as shown on Page 13.

5. **Backing**

 – cut the backing fabric into 2 equal length pieces.

 – remove the selvages and stitch the long sides of the 2 pieces together.

 – press the seam allowance.

6. **Marking** – if you wish to do quilting other than "in the ditch", mark the quilt at this time. Refer to Page 14.

7. **Sandwich** – prepare the quilt for quilting as shown on Page 15.

8. **Quilting** – machine or hand quilt as desired.

9. **Binding**

 – cut 8 strips of binding fabric 2 1/2" wide.

 – join 2 long strips together (using a bias join) for each side.

 – apply the binding following the directions on Page 16.

Circle of Love

All around the circle they go
And each of them already know,

With hearts below and up above
How precious is the gift of love,

For babes or friends this quilt will make
The memories of love for them to take,

With them forever the gift you gave
To hold, to cherish, remember and save.

The colour plates for 'Circle of Love' are shown on Page 29. The instructions and fabric requirements given are for a 1" finished grid. Find below a list of grid sizes and corresponding project sizes if you desire a size different than given in the instructions:

NOTE: The following grid sizes are for the finished size of the quilt **before** borders.

1/4"	Finished Grid	=	9 1/2" x 14"
1/2"	Finished Grid	=	14" x 28"
3/4"	Finished Grid	=	28 1/2" x 42"
1"	**Finished Grid**	**=**	**38" x 56"**
1 1/4"	Finished Grid	=	47" x 70"
1 1/2"	Finished Grid	=	57" x 84"

Grid Size: 1" Finished Grid

Quilt Size: 45" x 63" Including Borders

... Continued on Page 27

Circle of Love
QUILT

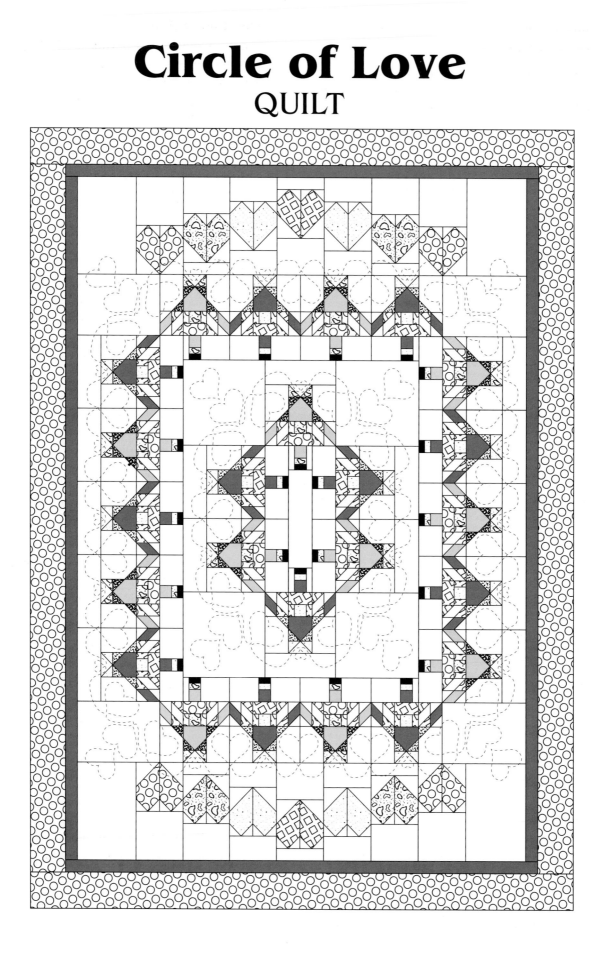

Continued from Page 25 ... Circle of Love

Fabric Requirements:

▨ 1/4 yd. (.25 m) Doll #1 – Bow, Socks,
Accent & 4 Hearts

▦ 1/8 yd. (.15 m) Doll #1 – Hair

▣ 1/4 yd. (.25 m) Doll #1 – Dress & 2 Hearts

☐ 1/3 yd. (.3 m) Doll #1 – Face, Arms, Legs

■ 1/8 yd. (.15 m) Doll #1 – Shoes

▢ 1/4 yd. (.25 m) Doll #2 – Bow, Socks,
Accent & 4 Hearts

▩ 1/8 yd. (.15 m) Doll #2 – Hair

◪ 1/4 yd. (.25 m) Doll #2 – Dress & 2 Hearts

▦ 1/3 yd. (.3 m) Doll #2 – Face, Arms, Legs

■ 1/8 yd. (.15 m) Doll #2 – Shoes

☐ 2 3/8 yd. (2.2 m) for Background

▨ 1/4 yd. (.25 m) for First Border

◪ 5/8 yd. (.6 m) for Second Border

Backing – The quilt should measure 45" x 63" when finished. If your backing fabric is 45" wide you need only 1 3/4 yd. (1.6 m). If piecing is required for one horizontal seam on the backing you will need 3 5/8 yd. (3.3 m).

Instructions:

1. There are 15 different units to complete for this quilt. Piece the required number of units following the General Instructions and using the cutting and piecing diagrams on Page 28. Refer to Page 9 for the correct sizes to cut for the 1" finished grid.

2. After the units are completed, lay them out following the quilt diagram on Page 26 as a guide.

   a) Sew the 2 rows of completed dolls for the sides.

   b) Sew the center section including the legs from the top and bottom dolls.

   c) Sew the top and bottom dolls bodies and heads in a row including the background pieces on each end of the row.

   d) Stitch the hearts together in a row including the background pieces at each end of the row.

3. **First Border** (1" finished)

   – cut 5 strips of first border fabric 1 1/2" wide.

   – cut 1 long strip in half.

   – cut 1 short strip to 1 long strip for each of the side borders.

   – one long strip each will suffice for the top and bottom borders.

   – apply borders using the Log Cabin Method as shown on Page 13.

4. **Second Border** (2 1/2" finished)

   – cut 7 strips of second border fabric 3" wide.

   – cut 2 long strips in half.

   – sew 2 long strips and 1 short strip together for each of the side borders.

   – sew 1 long strip and 1 short strip together for the top and bottom borders.

   – apply in the manner as the first border.

5. **Backing**

   – if your fabric is wide enough, you will just use one piece of fabric.

   – if you need to piece the backing, cut the purchased length into 2 equal length pieces.

   – remove the selvages and stitch the long edges of the 2 pieces together.

   – press the seam allowance.

6. **Marking**

   – a quilting template is provided at the beginning of the book.

   – mark the quilting design on the quilt top following the quilt diagram on Page 26 for placement.

7. **Sandwich** – prepare quilt for quilting as shown on Page 15.

8. **Quilting** – stitch the ditch around the dolls and the hearts.

   – machine or hand quilt the marked design.

9. **Binding**

   – cut 7 strips of binding fabrics 2 1/2" wide.

   – cut 2 long strips in half.

   – sew 1 long strip to 1 short strip for each of the four sides.

   – join them using a bias join.

   – apply the binding following the instruction on Page 16.

Circle of Love
Quilt

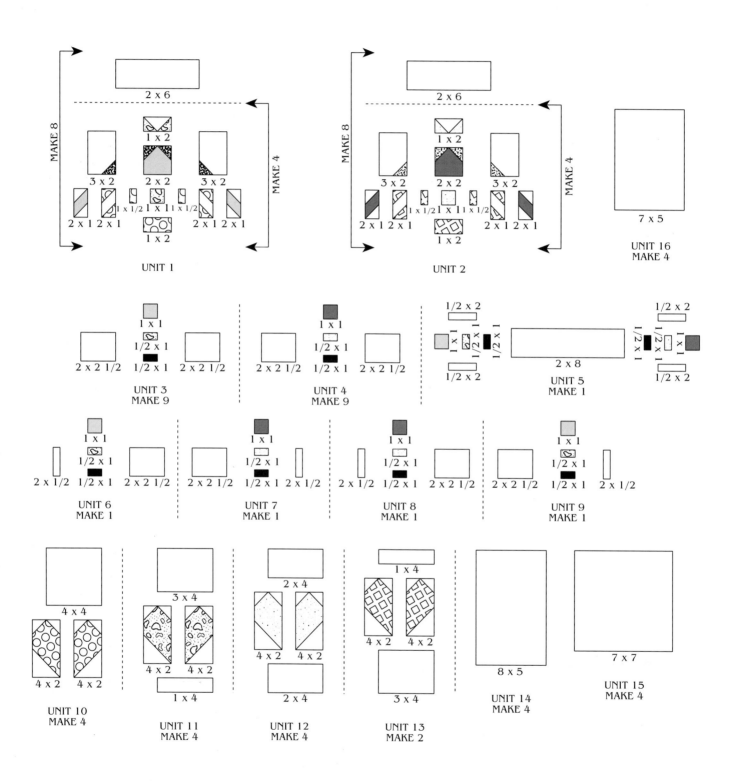

Circle of Love

Circle of Love
Quilt – 43" x 61"
by Betty Lawson
Calgary, Alberta

Circle of Love
Quilt – 43" x 61"
by Betty Lawson
Calgary, Alberta

Circle of Love
Quilt – 43" x 61"
Back Art
by Betty Lawson
Calgary, Alberta

Circle of Love
Quilt – 45" x 63"
by Melinda Brown
Bearly Stitchin' – Pasadena, California

Kitty Wall Hanging – 9" x 39"
by Darlene McCorrister
Darlene's Fabrics
Strathmore, Alberta

Rows 'n Bows

Rows 'n Bows
by Melinda Brown
Bearly Stitchin'
Pasadena, California
32" x 26"

Rows 'n Bows
by Sam Butterwick
Calgary, Alberta
48" x 39"

Rows 'n Bows
by Janet Samuels
Calgary, Alberta
32" x 26"

Detail of Rows 'n Bows
Featuring Button Eyes
and a Lamé Bow
by Janet Samuels
Calgary, Alberta

Kitty-Licious

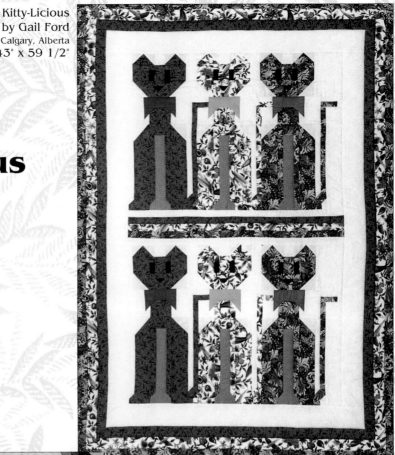

Kitty-Licious
by Gail Ford
Calgary, Alberta
43" x 59 1/2"

Kitty-Licious
by Bruce Webb
Sonora Yard Goods – Sonora, California
75" x 104" – Large Quilt 1 1/2" grid
14" x 20" – Small Quilt 1/4" grid

Quilted Paw Prints
by Lorraine Stangness
Strathmore, Alberta

Dino-Mite!
by Chris Basham
Bearly Stitchin' –
Pasadena, California
45" x 59"

Dino-Mite!

Dino-Mite! – 62" x 83"
Brontosaurus Joe – 42" x 31"
Pillow – 15 1/2" x 17"
Soft Sculpture – 22" x 22"
and Tote – 21 1/2" x 17"
by Lorraine Stangness
Strathmore, Alberta

Brontosaurus Joe
by Lorraine Stangness
Strathmore, Alberta
42" x 31"

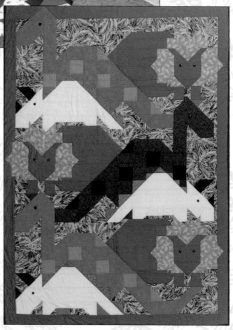

Dino-Mite!
by Sandy Wey
Calgary, Alberta
60" x 81"

Dino-Mite! Back Art
by Lorraine Stangness
Strathmore, Alberta
62" x 83"

Dino-Mite!

Dino-Mite!
by Joanne Baird and Caryl Yarmchuk
The Quilter's Cabin – Calgary, Alberta
41" x 55"

Detail of Gold and Black Ribbon
Prairie Points and Silver Lamé

Tote Bags by
Lorraine Stangness
Strathmore, Alberta
21 1/2" x 17"

& Other Things Nice

Bib by
Lorraine Stangness
Strathmore, Alberta

Navajo Friendship

Example of
Southwestern
Colour Scheme
by Lorraine Stangness
Strathmore, Alberta

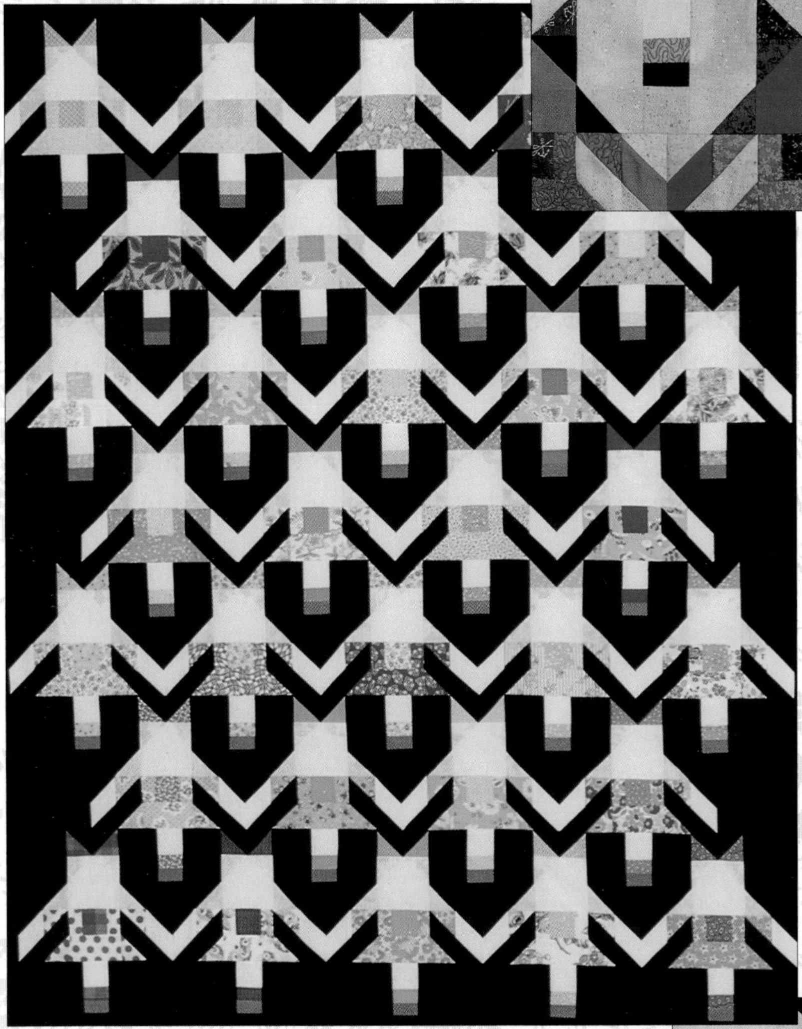

Navajo Friendship Quilt
by Cheryl Rosenquist
Sonora Yard Goods – Sonora, California
54" x 64 1/2"

1930's original and reproduction fabrics
were used in this quilt.

Doll-ightful!
Machine Quilting
by Lorraine Stangness
Strathmore, Alberta

Doll-ightful!

Doll-ightful Quilt and Wall Hanging
by Lorraine Stangness
Strathmore, Alberta
Quilt – 69 1/2" x 102 1/4"
Wall Hanging – 40 1/2" x 40 1/2"

TOP		
SECTION 5	SECTION 1	SECTION 5
SECTION 2	SECTION 3	SECTION 2
	SECTION 4	
	SECTION 3	
SECTION 5	SECTION 1	SECTION 5

Doll-ightful!
WALL HANGING

REMINDER:
Sizes refer to number of grids,
NOT measurements.
See Grid Conversion Chart Page 9.

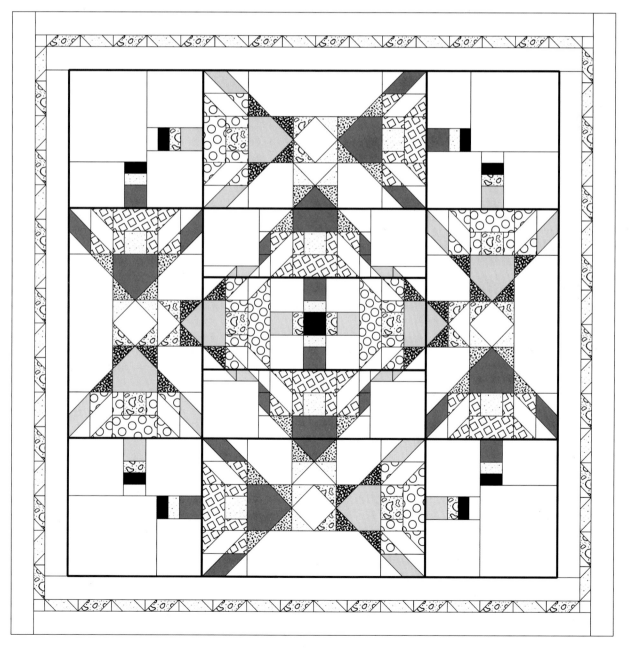

Doll-ightful!
Wall Hanging

SECTION 1
Make 2

SECTION 2
Make 2

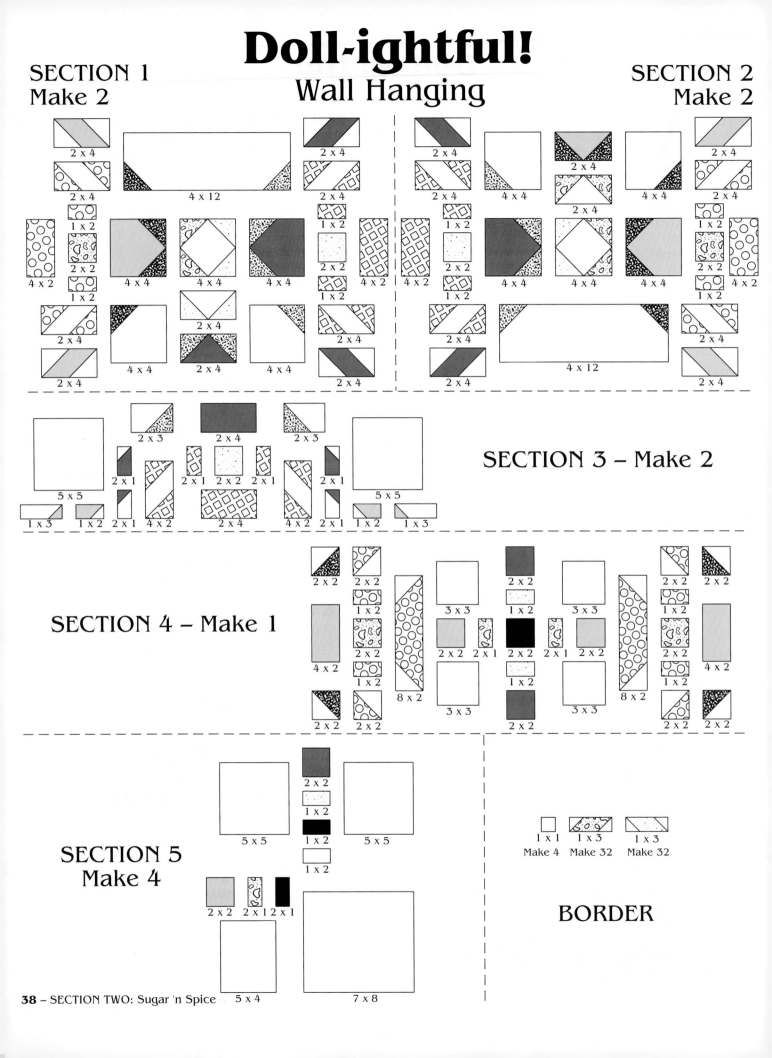

SECTION 3 – Make 2

SECTION 4 – Make 1

SECTION 5
Make 4

BORDER

1 x 1   1 x 3   1 x 3
Make 4   Make 32   Make 32

Doll-ightful!

A wall hanging with a difference! Circle in and circle out – these dolls create an interesting graphic design. The floating border adds the finishing touch to this wall hanging. See colour plate on Page 36.

The instructions and fabric requirements given below are for a 3/4" finished grid. Find below a list of wall hanging sizes if you desire a size different than given in the instructions.

1/4"	Finished Grid	=	13 1/2" x 13 1/2"
1/2"	Finished Grid	=	27" x 27"
3/4"	**Finished Grid**	**=**	**40 1/2" x 40 1/2"**
1"	Finished Grid	=	54" x 54"
1 1/4"	Finished Grid	=	67 1/2" x 67 1/2"
1 1/2"	Finished Grid	=	81" x 81"

Grid Size: 3/4" Finished Grid

Quilt Size: 40 1/2" x 40 1/2"

Fabric Requirements:

1/4 yd. (.25 m) Doll #1 – Bow, Socks, Accent & Border #1

1/4 yd. (.25 m) Doll #1 – Hair

1/4 yd. (.25 m) Doll #1 – Dress

1/3 yd. (.3 m) Doll #1 – Face, Arms, Legs

1/4 yd. (.25 m) Doll #2 – Bow, Socks, Accent & Border #2

1/4 yd. (.25 m) Doll #2 – Hair

1/4 yd. (.25 m) Doll #2 – Dress

1/3 yd. (.3 m) Doll #2 – Face, Arms, Legs

1/8 yd. (.15 m) Doll #2 – Shoes

1 3/4 yd. (1.6 m) for Background

1/3 yd. (.3 m) of Binding fabric

1 1/4 yd. (1.2 m) of Backing

Instructions:

1. Piece all the required sections following the General Instructions and using the cutting and piecing diagrams on Page 38. Refer to Page 9 for the correct sizes to cut for the 3/4" finished grid.

2. Layout the sections following the wall hanging layout diagram found on Page 37. Stitch. Press well.

3. **First Border** (Background)
   - cut 4 strips of fabric 2" wide.
   - follow the instructions on Page 13 for applying the first border Log Cabin Style.

4. **Pieced Border**
   - make the units shown on the cutting and piecing diagram on Page 38.
   - top and bottom borders

   Sew 8 units [diagram] to 8 units [diagram], twice. Remember to alternate units.

   - side borders

   Sew one background square, 8 units [diagram], 8 units [diagram] and one background square, twice. Remember to alternate units.

   - apply pieced borders as for first border.

5. **Second Border** (Background)
   - cut 4 strips of fabric 2" wide. Apply second border as for first border.

6. **Backing** – cut the backing fabric 42" x 42" (approximately 1 1/2" larger than the quilt top)

7. **Marking** – if you wish to do quilting other than "in the ditch" mark the quilt top at this time. Refer to Page 14.

8. **Sandwich** – prepare the quilt for quilting as shown on Page 15.

9. **Quilting** – machine or hand quilt as desired.

10. **Binding** – cut 4 strips of binding fabric 2 1/2" wide. Apply the binding as shown on Page 16.

NOTE: For other variations of this design to use for larger quilts, please refer to Section 4, The Five E's, Page 60 and Section Five: Diagrams, Page 64.

Dino-Mite!
QUILT

SECTION 1 SECTION 2 SECTION 3 SECTION 4 SECTION 5 SECTION 6 SECTION 7 SECTION 8

Dino-Mite!

Humps and bumps and lumps galore
This describes the dinosaur,

Large and majestic in his stand
Bumbling and stumbling through the land,

Oh! what fun to sew the sections
Easily making the corner connections,

Add backgrounds and borders and accents and such
Bright colours or not adds a personal touch,

Sew on and have fun with the DINO-MITE
Completing the quilt for a child's delight.

Colour plates of this quilt are shown on Pages 32 & 33. The directions and fabric require-ments given below are for a 3/4" finished grid. Find below a list of grid sizes and corresponding quilt sizes, if you desire a size different than given in the directions:

1/4"	Finished Grid =	28" x 35"
1/2"	Finished Grid =	45" x 59"
3/4"	**Finished Grid =**	**62" x 83"**
1"	Finished Grid =	79" x 107"
1 1/4"	Finished Grid =	96" x 120"

Grid Size: 3/4" Finished Grid
Quilt Size: 62" x 83"

Fabric Requirements:

3/4 yd. (.7 m) – Dinosaur #1

1/4 yd. (.25 m) – Dinosaur #1, Spots

1 yd. (1 m) – Dinosaur #2, Body & Face

5/8 yd. (.6 m) – Dinosaur #3

1/2 yd. (.5 m) – Dinosaur #4

1/4 yd. (.25 m) – Dinosaur #4, Spots

1/2 yd. (.5 m) – Dinosaur #2, Mane

1/4 yd. (.25 m) – Dinosaur #2 & #3, Humps

1/8 yd. (.15 m) – Dinosaur #3, Horns

1 1/4 yd. (1.2 m) for Background

7/8 yd. (.8 m) of Inside Border Fabric

1/3 yd.	(.3 m)	1st Folded Narrow Border
5/8 yd.	(.6 m)	2nd Border
7/8 yd.	(.8 m)	3rd Border
3 3/4 yd.	(3.4 m)	Backing Fabric
5/8 yd.	(.6 m)	Binding Fabric

Instructions:

1. Piece the dinosaurs following the General Instructions and using the cutting and piecing diagrams on Pages 42 to 49. Refer to the Grid Conversion Chart on Page 9 for the correct sizes to cut for the 3/4" finished grid.

2. Stitch the eight completed sections together as shown on the quilt layout diagram on Page 40.

3. Narrow Folded Border

   – cut 7 strips 1 1/2" wide.

   – stitch 2 strips together for each side.

   – stitch 1 1/2 strips together for the top and for the bottom.

   – press these strips in half lengthwise, WRONG SIDES TOGETHER.

   – measure the length of the quilt body as shown on Page 13. Cut the 2 side folded border pieces to this measurement. Pin to the sides of the quilt body, matching centers and raw edges. Stitch. Do NOT press over.

   – measure the width of the quilt with side borders as shown on Page 13. Cut the remaining 2 sewn border pieces to this measurement. Pin to the top and bottom of the quilt, matching centers and raw edges even. Do NOT press over.

... Continued on Page 50

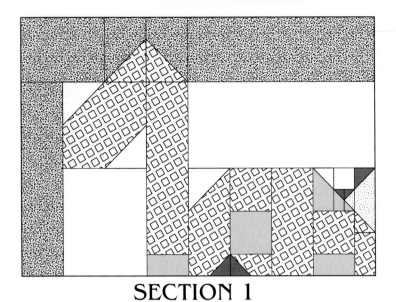

Dino-Mite!
SECTION 1
Quilt

SECTION 1

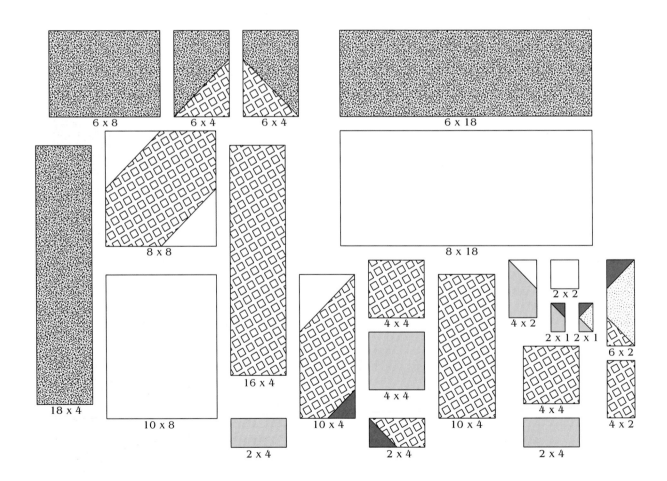

6 x 8

6 x 4

6 x 4

6 x 18

8 x 18

8 x 8

16 x 4

18 x 4

10 x 8

2 x 4

10 x 4

2 x 4

4 x 4

4 x 4

10 x 4

2 x 4

2 x 2

4 x 2

2 x 1 2 x 1

6 x 2

4 x 4

4 x 2

Dino-Mite!
SECTION 2
Quilt

REMINDER:
Sizes refer to number of grids, **NOT** measurements. See Grid Conversion Chart Page 9.

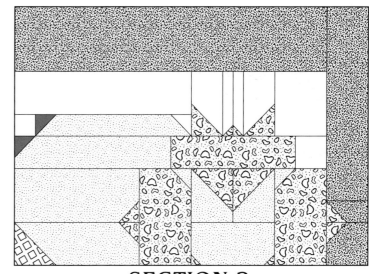

SECTION 2

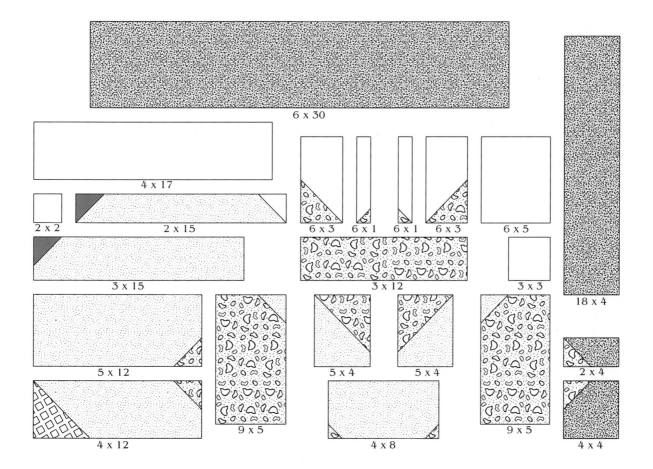

6 x 30

4 x 17

2 x 2

2 x 15

6 x 3   6 x 1   6 x 1   6 x 3   6 x 5

3 x 15

3 x 12

3 x 3

18 x 4

5 x 12

5 x 4   5 x 4

2 x 4

9 x 5

4 x 12

4 x 8

9 x 5

4 x 4

Dino-Mite!
SECTION 3
Quilt

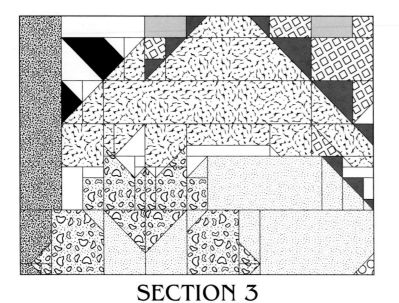

SECTION 3

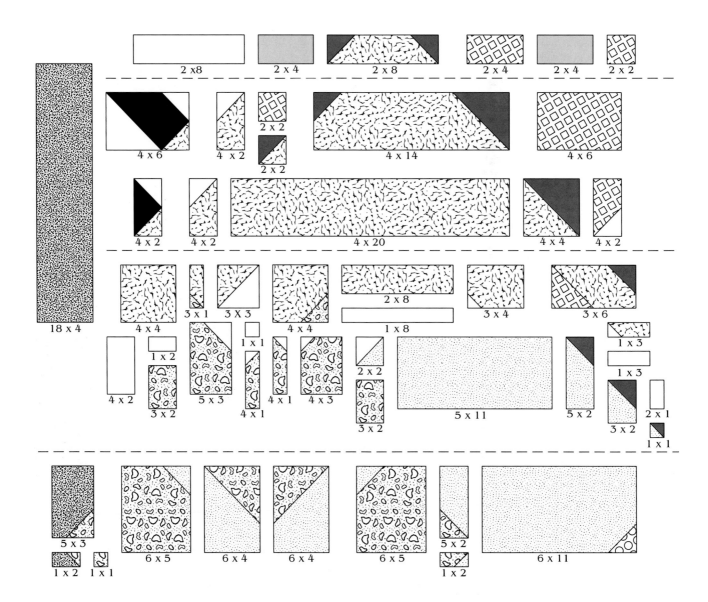

2 x8   2 x 4   2 x 8   2 x 4   2 x 4   2 x 2

4 x 6   4 x 2   2 x 2   4 x 14   4 x 6

2 x 2

4 x 2   4 x 2   4 x 20   4 x 4   4 x 2

3 x 1   3 x 3   2 x 8   3 x 4   3 x 6

18 x 4   4 x 4   1 x 1   4 x 4   1 x 8   1 x 3

1 x 2   1 x 3

4 x 2   5 x 3   2 x 2   5 x 11   5 x 2   2 x 1

3 x 2   4 x 1   4 x 3   3 x 2

4 x 1   3 x 2   1 x 1

5 x 3   6 x 5   6 x 4   6 x 4   6 x 5   5 x 2   6 x 11

1 x 2   1 x 1   1 x 2

Dino-Mite!
SECTION 4
Quilt

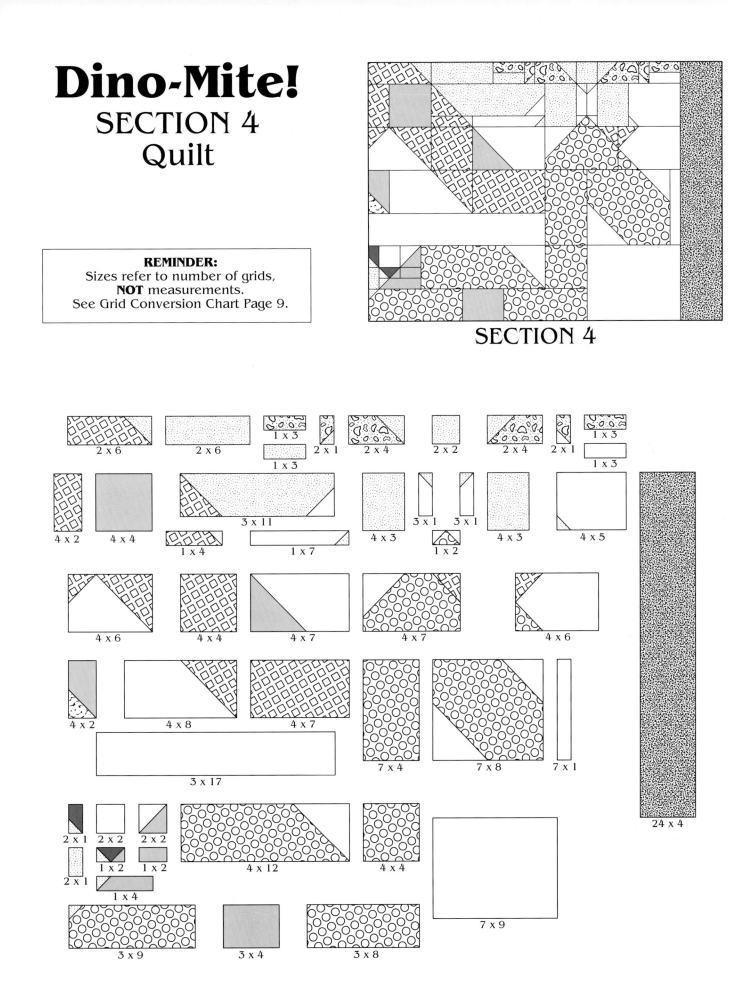

SECTION 4

2 x 6   2 x 6   1 x 3   2 x 1   2 x 4   2 x 2   2 x 4   2 x 1   1 x 3
        1 x 3   1 x 3

4 x 2   4 x 4   3 x 11   4 x 3   3 x 1 3 x 1   4 x 3   4 x 5
        1 x 4   1 x 7   1 x 2

4 x 6   4 x 4   4 x 7   4 x 7   4 x 6

4 x 2   4 x 8   4 x 7   7 x 4   7 x 8   7 x 1

3 x 17

2 x 1 2 x 2 2 x 2   4 x 12   4 x 4

1 x 2 1 x 2

2 x 1

1 x 4   7 x 9

24 x 4

3 x 9   3 x 4   3 x 8

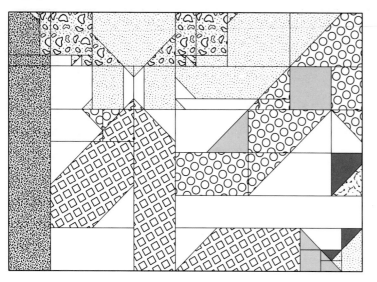

Dino-Mite!
SECTION 5
Quilt

SECTION 5

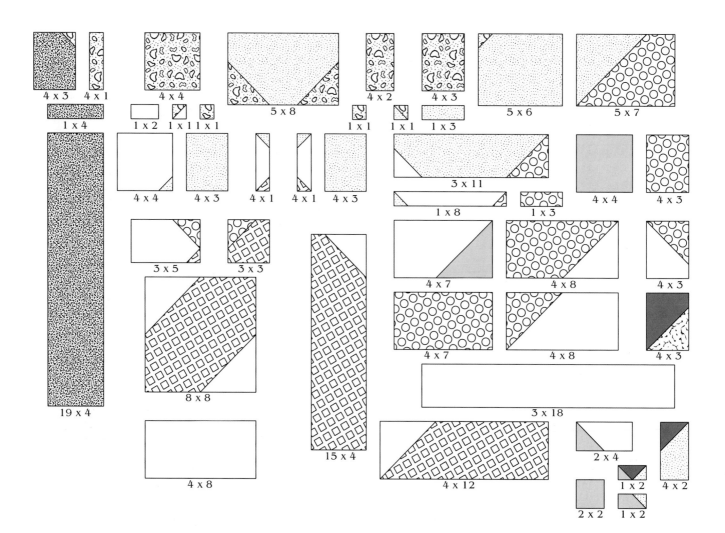

4 x 3   4 x 1   4 x 4   4 x 2   4 x 3   5 x 6   5 x 7

1 x 4   1 x 2 1 x 1 1 x 1   5 x 8   1 x 1   1 x 1   1 x 3

4 x 4   4 x 3   4 x 1 4 x 1 4 x 3   3 x 11   4 x 4   4 x 3

                                                                1 x 8   1 x 3

3 x 5   3 x 3   4 x 7   4 x 8   4 x 3

19 x 4   4 x 7   4 x 8   4 x 3

                    8 x 8   3 x 18

                                        15 x 4

        4 x 8   4 x 12   2 x 4

                                                                    1 x 2   4 x 2

                                                            2 x 2   1 x 2

Dino-Mite!
SECTION 6
Quilt

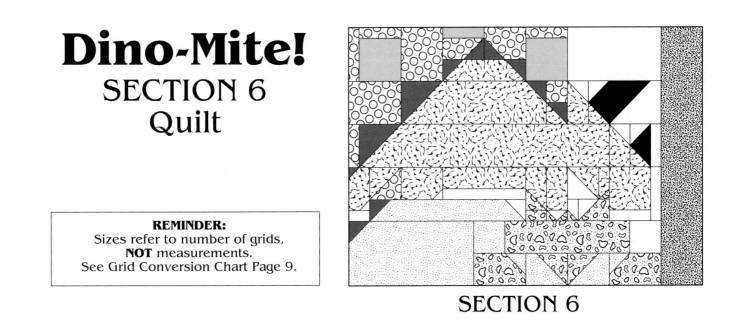

SECTION 6

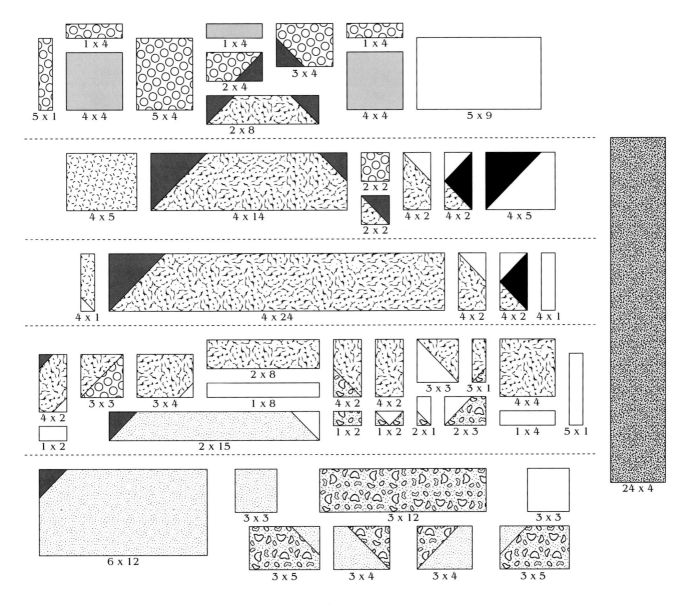

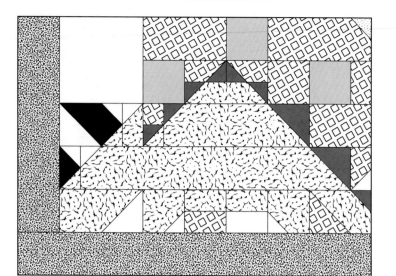

Dino-Mite!
SECTION 7
Quilt

SECTION 7

REMINDER:
Sizes refer to number of grids,
NOT measurements.
See Grid Conversion Chart Page 9.

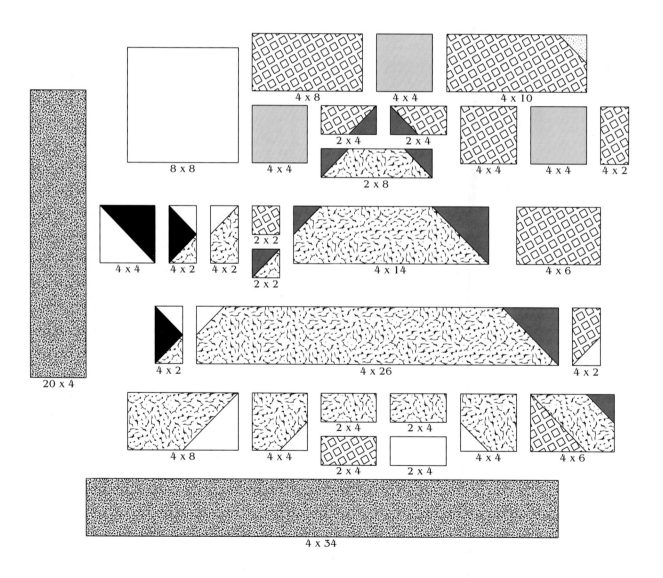

Dino-Mite!
SECTION 8
Quilt

REMINDER:
Sizes refer to number of grids,
NOT measurements.
See Grid Conversion Chart Page 9.

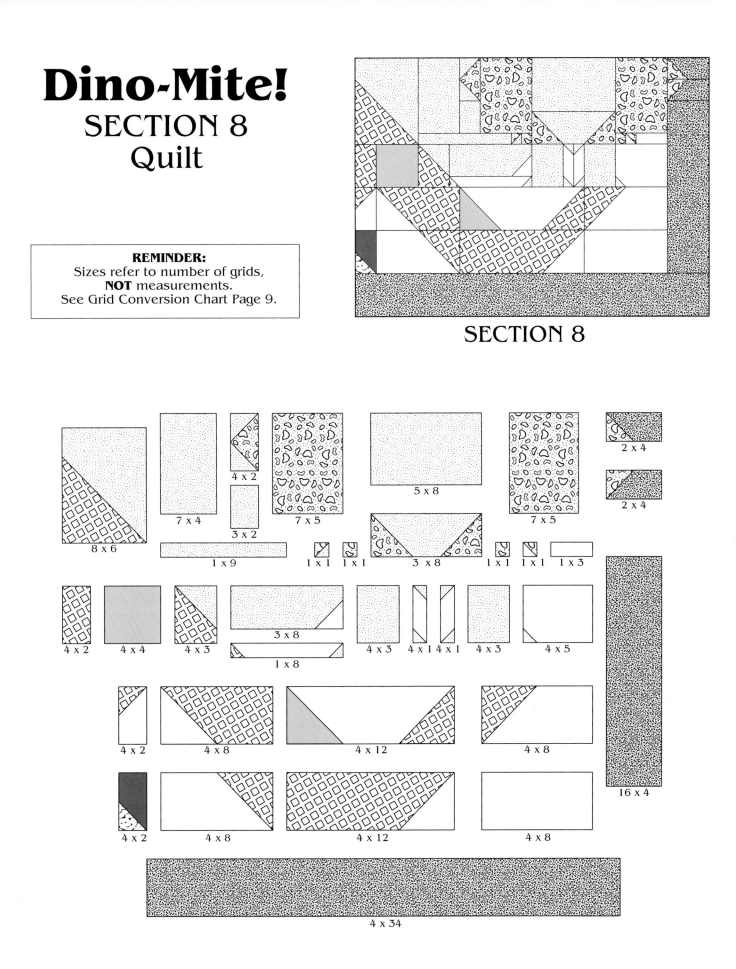

SECTION 8

8 x 6

7 x 4

4 x 2

3 x 2

7 x 5

5 x 8

7 x 5

2 x 4

2 x 4

1 x 9

1 x 1

1 x 1

3 x 8

1 x 1

1 x 1

1 x 3

4 x 2

4 x 4

4 x 3

3 x 8

1 x 8

4 x 3

4 x 1

4 x 1

4 x 3

4 x 5

4 x 2

4 x 8

4 x 12

4 x 8

16 x 4

4 x 2

4 x 8

4 x 12

4 x 8

4 x 34

Continued from Page 41... Dino-Mite!

4. **First Outside Border**

   – cut 7 strips 2 1/2" wide.

   – stitch 2 strips together for each side.

   – stitch 1 1/2 strips together for the top and for the bottom.

   – apply borders as shown on Page 13.

5. **Second Outside Border**

   – cut 7 strips 4" wide.

   – stitch 2 strips together for each side.

   – stitch 1 1/2 strips together for the top and for the bottom.

   – apply in the same manner as First Outside Border.

6. **Backing**

   – cut the backing into two equal length pieces.

   – remove the selvages and stitch the long sides of the 2 pieces together.

   – press the seam allowances.

7. **Marking** – mark the desired quilting design on top of the quilt. See Page 14.

8. **Sandwich** – prepare the quilt for quilting as shown on Page 15.

9. **Quilting** – machine or hand quilt as desired.

10. **Binding** – cut 7 strips of binding fabric 2 1/2" wide. Join pieces as needed following the directions on Page 16. Apply the binding as shown on Page 16.

Brontosaurus Joe
WALL HANGING

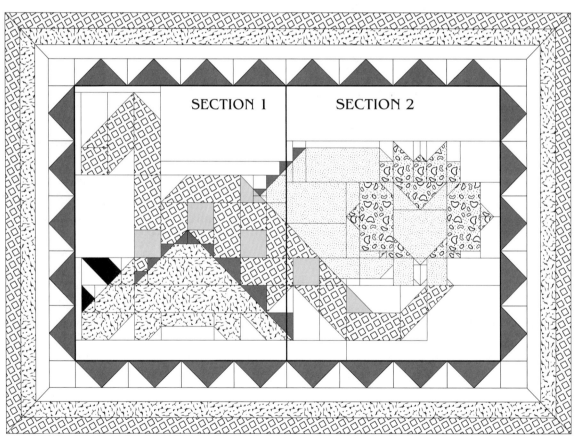

Three little dinosaurs all in a row,
Maybe you could name one Brontosaurus Joe!
Choose the one you like the best,
And he will guard you while you rest!

Brontosaurus Joe

Colour plate of wall hanging is shown on Page 32. The instructions and fabric requirements given below are for a 1/2" finished grid. Find below a list of grid sizes and corresponding project sizes if you desire a size different than given in the instructions.

These grid sizes are for the finished sizes of Section 1 and 2 **before** borders are added.

1/4"	Finished Grid	= 21 1/2" x 15 1/2"
1/2"	**Finished Grid**	**= 42" x 31"**
3/4"	Finished Grid	= 64 1/2" x 46 1/2"
1"	Finished Grid	= 86" x 62"

Grid Size: 1/2" Finished Grid

Quilt Size: 43" x 31" Including Borders

Fabric Requirements:

5/8 yd. (.6 m) – Dinosaur #1 & 3rd Border

1/8 yd. (.15 m) – Dinosaur #1, Spots

3/8 yd. (.35 m) – Dinosaur #2, Body & Face

3/8 yd. (.35 m) – Dinosaur #2, Mane

1/2 yd. (.5 m) – Dinosaur #3 & 2nd Border

1/8 yd. (.15 m) – Dinosaur #3, Horns

1/2 yd. (.5 m) – Dinosaur #2 & 3,
Humps & Pieced Border

1 1/2 yd. (1.4 m) for Background,
Pieced Border & 1st Border

1 yd. (.9 m) of Backing

1/3 yd. (.3 m) of Binding fabric

Instructions:

1. Piece the dinosaurs following the General Instructions and using the cutting and piecing diagrams on Page 52 and 53. Refer to Page 9 for the correct sizes to cut for the 1/2" finished grid.

2. Stitch the two completed sections together as shown on the wall hanging layout diagram on Page 51.

3. **Pieced Border**

   – cut 26 strips of the accent fabric 2 1/2" x 4 1/2".

   – cut 56 pieces of background fabric 2 1/2" x 2 1/2".

– stitch 26 units:

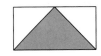

Refer to General Instructions for Piecing Technique

– stitch the following rows:

Top	–	8 units
Bottom	–	8 units
1st Side	–	1 – 2 1/2" x 2 1/2" Background Square,
		5 units,
		1 – 2 1/2" x 2 1/2" Background Square
2nd Side	–	1 – 2 1/2" x 2 1/2" Background Square,
		5 units,
		1 – 2 1/2" x 2 1/2" Background Square

4. **Mitered Borders**

   – cut 4 strips from Border Fabric #1 – 1 3/4" wide.

   – cut 4 strips from Border Fabric #2 – 1 1/2" wide.

   – cut 4 strips from Border Fabric #3 - 1 3/4" wide.

   – stitch one strip of each border fabric together lengthwise to form 4 strip sets.

   – apply the borders and miter the corners as shown on Page 13.

5. **Backing** – cut the backing fabric 45" x 34" (approximately 1 1/2" larger than the quilt top)

6. **Marking** – if you wish to do quilting other than "in the ditch" mark the quilt top at this time. Refer to Page 14.

7. **Sandwich** – prepare the quilt for quilting as shown on Page 15.

8. **Quilting** – machine or hand quilt as desired.

9. **Binding** – cut 4 strips of binding fabric 2 1/2" wide. Apply the binding as shown on Page 16.

Brontosaurus Joe
SECTION 1
Wall Hanging

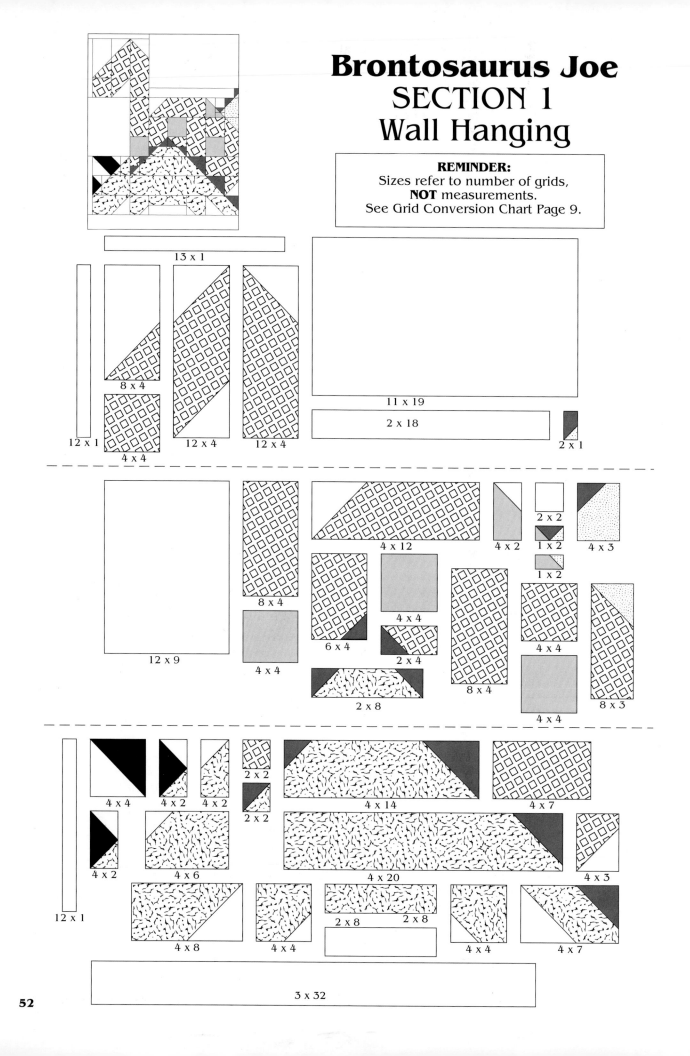

REMINDER:
Sizes refer to number of grids,
NOT measurements.
See Grid Conversion Chart Page 9.

13 x 1

8 x 4

12 x 1

4 x 4

12 x 4

12 x 4

11 x 19

2 x 18

2 x 1

12 x 9

8 x 4

4 x 4

6 x 4

4 x 12

2 x 4

2 x 8

4 x 4

4 x 4

8 x 4

2 x 2

4 x 2

1 x 2

1 x 2

4 x 3

4 x 4

8 x 3

12 x 1

4 x 4

4 x 2

4 x 2

2 x 2

2 x 2

4 x 14

4 x 7

4 x 2

4 x 6

4 x 20

4 x 3

4 x 8

4 x 4

2 x 8

2 x 8

4 x 4

4 x 7

3 x 32

Brontosaurus Joe
SECTION 2
Wall Hanging

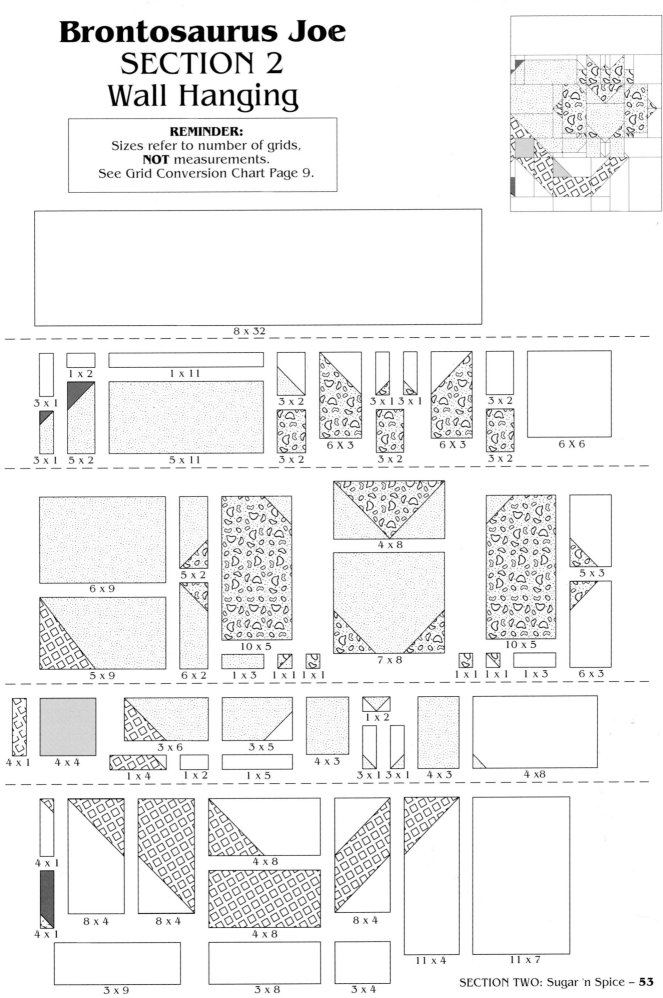

8 x 32

3 x 1

1 x 2

1 x 11

3 x 2

3 x 1 3 x 1

3 x 2

6 X 6

3 x 1

5 x 2

5 x 11

3 x 2

6 x 3

3 x 2

6 X 3

3 x 2

6 x 9

5 x 2

10 x 5

4 x 8

7 x 8

10 x 5

5 x 3

5 x 9

6 x 2

1 x 3   1 x 1   1 x 1

1 x 1   1 x 1   1 x 3

6 x 3

4 x 1

4 x 4

3 x 6

3 x 5

1 x 2

4 x 3

4 x 3

4 x8

1 x 4

1 x 2

1 x 5

3 x 1 3 x 1

4 x 1

4 x 8

4 x 8

8 x 4

4 x 1

8 x 4

8 x 4

4 x 8

8 x 4

11 x 4

11 x 7

3 x 9

3 x 8

3 x 4

BIBS, PILLOW FRONTS & SOFT SCULPTURES

REMINDER:
Sizes refer to number of grids,
NOT measurements.
See Grid Conversion Chart
Page 9.

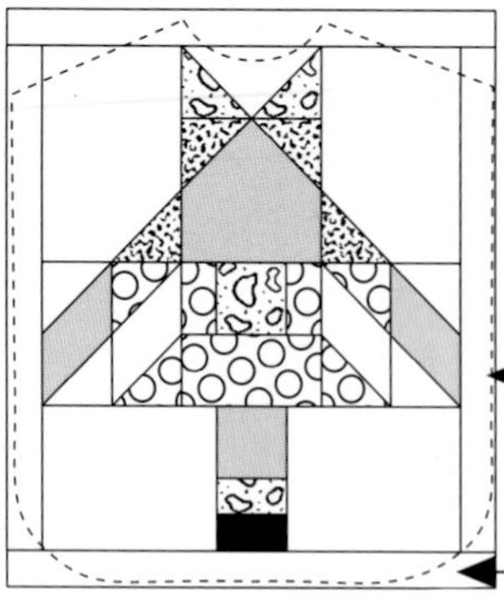

Bib

Soft Sculpture &
Wallhanging

14 x 16

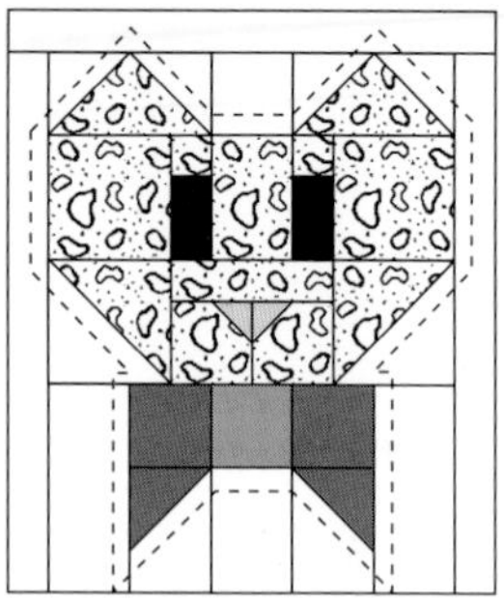

12 x 15

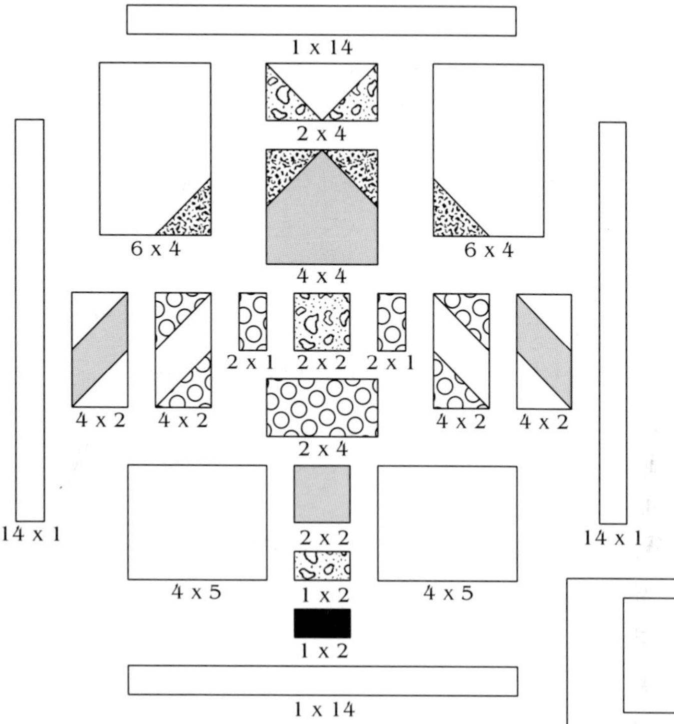

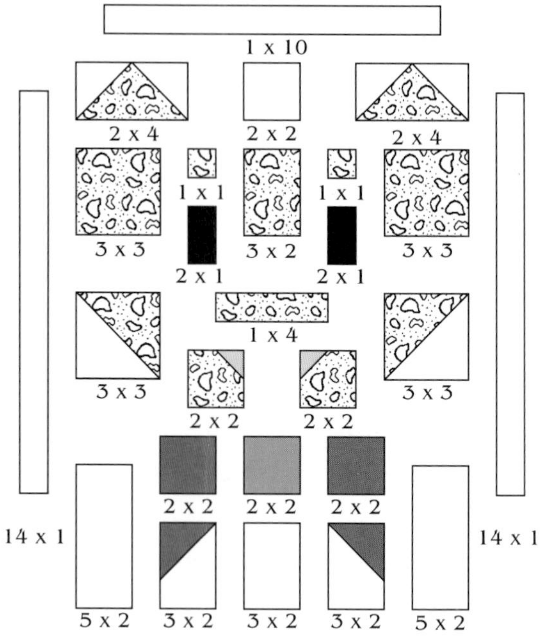

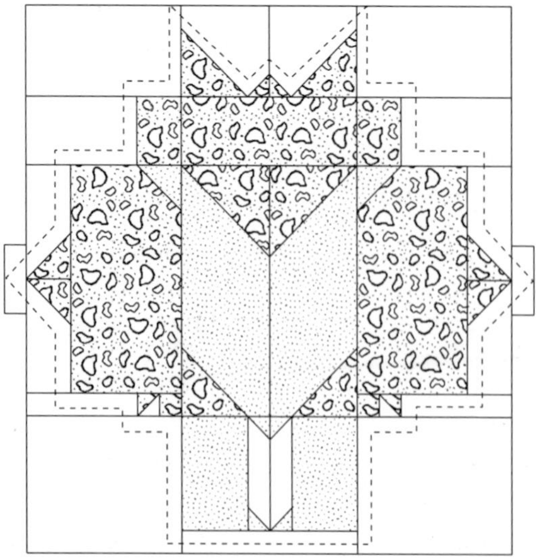

1 x 14

2 x 4

6 x 4

4 x 4

6 x 4

2 x 1 2 x 2 2 x 1

4 x 2   4 x 2

2 x 4

4 x 2   4 x 2

14 x 1

4 x 5

2 x 2

1 x 2

1 x 2

4 x 5

14 x 1

1 x 14

1 x 10

2 x 4   2 x 2   2 x 4

3 x 3 1 x 1 3 x 3 1 x 1 3 x 3

2 x 1   2 x 1

1 x 4

3 x 3   3 x 3

2 x 2   2 x 2

14 x 1

2 x 2   2 x 2   2 x 2

14 x 1

5 x 2 3 x 2 3 x 2 3 x 2 5 x 2

4 x 7   4 x 4   4 x 4   4 x 7

3 x 5   3 x 2   3 x 8   3 x 2   3 x 5

5 x 2

3 x 1

5 x 2   10 x 5   11 x 4   11 x 4   10 x 5

5 x 2

3 x 1

1 x 5   1 x 1 1 x 1   1 x 1 1 x 1   1 x 5

24 x 22

6 x 7

5 x 3 5 x 1 5 x 1 5 x 3

1 x 8

6 x 7

54 – SECTION THREE: & Other Things Nice

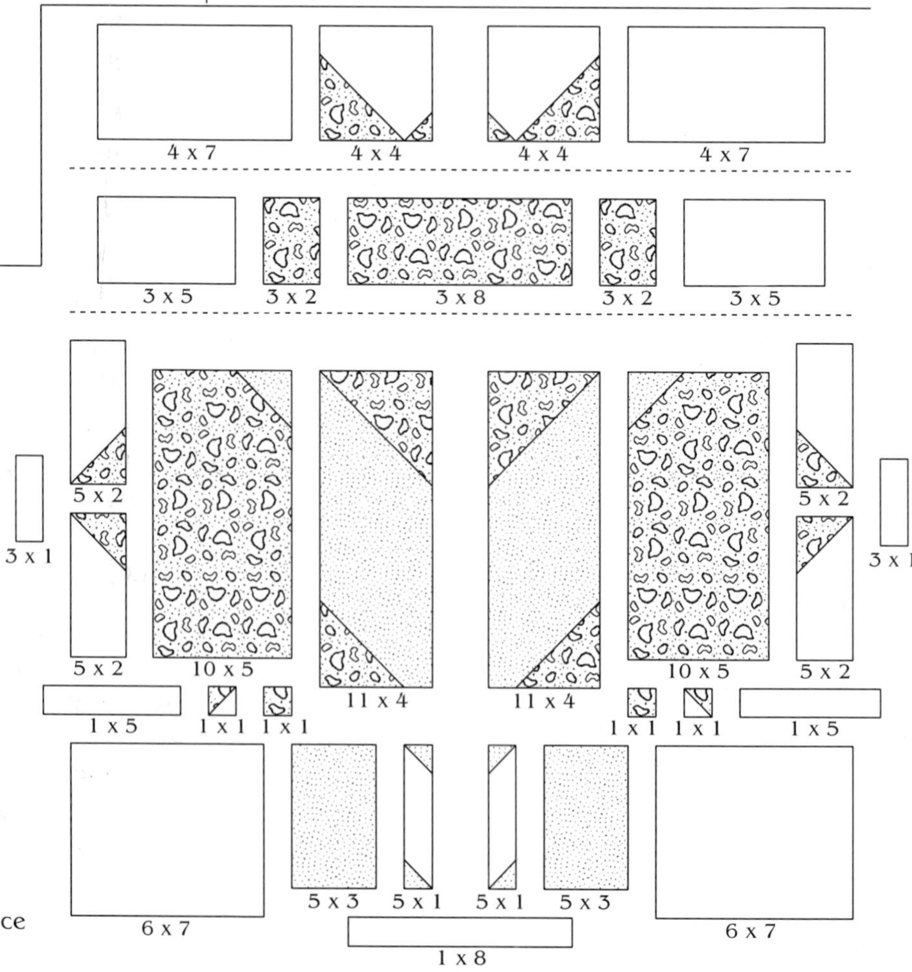

SECTION THREE:
& Other Things Nice

There's been Sugar 'n Spice and now there's Other Things Nice! This section has been designed for smaller projects to compliment the quilts and wall hangings from the Sugar 'n Spice section.

The Other Things Nice section gives you the choice of sewing bibs, accent pillow or pajama pillow, soft sculpture or a tote bag utilizing the designs for the Doll, the Dinosaur or the Kittens. The piecing diagrams for these projects are shown on Page 54. Each of the projects use the same piecing diagrams but each uses a different finished grid size. Individual instructions and fabric requirements for each project are given on the following pages:

A. The Bibs
Fabric Requirements and Grid Size

1. THE DOLL BIB

Grid Size: 3/4" Finished Grid
Bib Size: 10 1/2" x 12" (approximately)
Fabric Requirements:

- 1 piece – 2" x 10" for Bow, Socks & Accent
- 1 piece – 2" x 10" for Hair
- 1 piece – 2" x 16" for Dress
- 1 piece – 3 1/2" x 10" for Face, Arms, Legs
- 1 piece – 2" x 2" for Shoes
- 1/4 yd. (.25 m) – Background & Ties
  - 1 piece – 12" x 14" of Backing
  - 1 piece – 12" x 14" of Batting (optional)

2. THE DINOSAUR BIB

Grid Size: 1/2" Finished Grid
Bib Size: 12" x 11" (approximately)
Fabric Requirements:

- 1 strip – 4 1/2" wide for Body & Face
- 1 strip – 3" wide for Mane
- 1/4 yd. (.25 m) for Background & Ties
  - 1 piece – 14" x 13" of Backing
  - 1 piece – 14" x 13" of Batting (optional)

3. THE KITTEN BIB

Grid Size: 3/4" Finished Grid

Bib Size: 10 1/2" x 12" (approximately)
Fabric Requirements:

- 1 strip – 4 3/4" wide for Face
- 1 piece – 2" x 2" for Knot on Bow Tie
- 1 strip – 2" wide for Bow Tie
- 1 piece – 2" x 3" for Eyes
- 1 piece – 1 1/4" x 3" for Nose
- 1/4 yd. (.25 m) – Background & Ties
  - 1 piece – 14" x 12" of Backing
  - 1 piece – 14" x 12" of Batting (optional)

B. The Bibs – Instructions:

1. Piece the front of the bib following the chart on Page 54. Refer to Page 9 for the correct sizes to cut for the bib you have chosen.

2. Cut the Bib Shape – draw the bib shape on the right side of the bib using the dotted lines on the diagrams as a guide. Cut the bib on this drawn line.

3. Ties – cut 2 pieces of tie fabric, 1 1/2" x 18". Fold each one in half lengthwise, stitch across one end and down the length, raw edges even.

Turn the ties to the right side using a turning tool.

4. Lay the ties on the right side of the bib front at the points and pin. Make sure the ties are out of the way of the seam allowance and secure.

5. Lay the bib front RIGHT SIDES TOGETHER with the backing piece. (Do NOT cut the backing.) If you wish to put batting in the bib, lay the piece of batting beneath the WRONG SIDE of the backing fabric. Pin all layers. Beginning at the bottom of the bib 1 1/2" from the center, begin stitching with a 1/4" seam allowance all around. Use the cut bib front as the seam guide. End stitching 1 1/2" from the center.

6. Turn the bib to the right side through the 3" opening. Hand stitch the opening.

7. If you have added batting, quilt as desired.

C. The Accent Pillow/Pajama Pillow Fabric Requirements and Grid Size

1. THE DOLL PILLOW

Grid Size: 1" Finished Grid

Pillow Size: 14" x 16" (Plus Ruffle)

Fabric Requirements:

- 1 piece – 2 1/2" x 9" for Bow, Socks & Accent
- 1 piece – 2 1/2" x 12" for Hair
- 1 piece – 2 1/2" x 20" for Dress
- 1 piece – 4 1/2" x 14" for Face, Arms, Legs
- 1 piece – 1 1/2" x 2 1/2" for Shoes
- 1/4 yd. (.25 m) – Background & Ties

    1 piece – 18" x 18" Lining for Pillow
    1 yard   (.9 m) Backing and Ruffle
    1 piece – 18" x 18" of Batting
    16" (45 cm.) Zipper

2. THE DINOSAUR PILLOW

Grid Size: 3/4" Finished Grid

Pillow Size: 16 1/2" x 18" (Plus Ruffle)

Fabric Requirements:

- 1 strip – 5 1/2" wide for Body & Face
- 1 strip – 7" wide for Mane
- 1/4 yd. (.25 m) for Background & Ties
    1 piece – 20" x 20" Lining for Pillow
    1 yard (.9 m) Backing and Ruffle
    1 piece – 20" x 20" of Batting
    18" (50 cm.) Zipper

3. THE KITTEN PILLOW

Grid Size: 1" Finished Grid

Pillow Size: 14" x 16" (Plus Ruffle)

Fabric Requirements:

- 1 strip – 6" wide for Face
- 1 piece – 2 1/2" x 2 1/2" for Knot on Bow Tie
- 1 piece – 2 1/2" x 15" wide for Bow Tie
- 1 piece – 2 1/2" x 3" for Eyes
- 1 piece – 1 1/2" x 3" for Nose
- 1/4 yd. (.25 m) – Background & Ties

    1 piece – 18" x 16" Lining for Pillow
    1 yard (.9 m) Backing and Ruffle
    1 piece – 18" x 16" of Batting
    16" (45 cm.) Zipper

D. The Accent Pillow/Pajama Pillow – Instructions:

1. Piece the pillow front following the chart on Page 54. Refer to Page 9 for the correct sizes to cut for the pillow you have chosen.

2. Lay the pillow front: lining piece WRONG SIDE UP, batting then pillow front RIGHT SIDE UP.

3. **Quilting the Pillow Front**
   - pin the three layers together.
   - quilt as desired.
   - cut the batting and lining even with the front pillow.

4. a) **Ruffle**
   - cut 3 strips 6 1/2" wide.
   - stitch the 3 strips together end for end.
   - fold the ruffle in half WRONG SIDES TOGETHER and press.
   - zig zag over a gathering cord close to the raw edges of the ruffle.
   - divide the ruffle into 4 equal lengths and mark with pins.

   b) **Attaching the Ruffle**
   - find the mid-point of each side of the pillow front and mark with a pin.
   - match the four divisions of the ruffle to the four divisions of the pillow front.
   - pin the ruffle to the pillow front RIGHT SIDES TOGETHER.
   - pull the gathering cord between the pins and gather the ruffle to fit the pillow front leaving more fullness at the corners.
   - stitch the ruffle to the pillow front.

5. **Pillow Back**
   - cut 2 pieces for the back of the pillow:

Doll	– 2	7 1/2" x 16 1/2"
Dinosaur	– 2	9 3/4" x 18 1/2"
Kitten	– 2	7 1/2" x 16 1/2"

   - fold to the WRONG SIDE 1/4" on the long side of both pieces. Press.
   - lay the zipper under the 2 folded edges, pin in place and stitch 1/8" from the folded edge of the fabric.

6. **Finishing the Pillow**
   - lay the pillow back (leave zipper open slightly) RIGHT SIDES TOGETHER on the pillow front and ruffle.
   - pin all raw edges even, stitch all around.

– turn the pillow to the RIGHT SIDE through the zipper opening.

7. **Accent Pillow or Pajama Pillow**
   – leave the pillow as is for the pajama pillow.
   – make a filler pillow and insert through the zipper opening for the accent pillow.

E. The Soft Sculpture Fabric Requirements and Grid Size

1. THE DOLL SOFT SCULPTURE

Grid Size: 1 1/4" Finished Grid

Sculpture Size: 17 1/2" x 20"

Fabric Requirements:

1 piece – 3" x 14" for Bow, Socks & Accent

1 piece – 3" x 15" for Hair

1 piece – 3" x 21" for Dress

1 piece – 5 1/2" x 14" for Face, Arms, Legs

1 piece – 3" x 3" for Shoes

1/2 yd. (.5 m) – Background

1 piece – 18" x 21" of Backing

1 piece – 18" x 21" of Batting

2. THE DINOSAUR SOFT SCULPTURE

Grid Size: 1" Finished Grid

Sculpture Size: 24" x 22"

Fabric Requirements:

1/3 yd. (.3 m) for Body & Face

1/3 yd. (.3 m) for Mane

3/8 yd. (.35 m) for Background

1 piece – 26" x 24" of Backing

1 piece – 26" x 24" of Batting

3. THE KITTEN SOFT SCULPTURE

Grid Size: 1 1/4" Finished Grid

Sculpture Size: 17 1/2" x 20"

Fabric Requirements:

1/4 yd. (.25 m) for Face

1 piece – 3" x 3" for Knot on Bow Tie

1 piece – 3" x 18" for Bow Tie

1 piece – 3" x 4" for Eyes

1 piece – 1 3/4" x 4" for Nose

3/8 yd. (.35 m) – Background

1 piece – 21" x 19" of Backing

1 piece – 21" x 19" of Batting

F. The Soft Sculpture – Instructions

1. Piece the soft sculpture front following the diagram on Page 54. Refer to Page 9 for the correct sizes to cut for the soft sculpture you have chosen.

2. Cut the front to the shape desired or use the dotted lines on the diagrams as a guideline.

3. Lay the soft sculpture front RIGHT SIDES TOGETHER with the backing piece. (Do NOT cut the backing.) Lay the batting under the backing piece and pin through all layers. Beginning at the bottom of the soft sculpture 1 1/2" from the center, begin stitching with a 1/4" seam allowance all around. Use the cut soft sculpture front as the seam guide. End the stitching 1 1/2" from the center.

4. Turn the soft sculpture to the right side through the 3" opening. Hand stitch the opening.

5. Quilt as desired.

G. The Tote
Fabric Requirements for Piece Work
   – 2 times what is stated for the piecework of the bibs.

Fabric Requirements for Tote

1 3/4 yd.	(1.7 m)	inside bag, lining 2 inside pockets, lining 2 outside pockets, bindings on 2 outside pockets
3/4 yd.	(.7 m)	outside bag
1 1/4 yd.	(1.25 m)	straps, 2 inside pockets, binding for top of bag
3/8 yd.	(.35 m)	zippered inside pocket
1 – 8"		piece of velcro
1 – 20"	(50 cm)	zipper
1	24" x 44"	piece of thick quilt batting
2	14" x 14"	pieces of thick quilt batting
2	2" x 60"	pieces of thick quilt batting

NOTE: The outside pockets are pieced the same as the bibs for the doll, the kitten and the dinosaur. Use the same grid sizes as for the bibs but DO NOT CUT after piecing – leave as a square.

H. The Tote – Instructions

1. **Cutting Instructions** – See Diagram 37 on Page 58.

2. Piece the outside pockets of your choice. Lay the outside pocket lining pieces WRONG SIDE UP. Lay one 14" square of batting on each of the lining pieces. Lay the pieced pockets on the batting RIGHT SIDE UP. Pin the 3 layers and quilt as desired.

Diagram #37

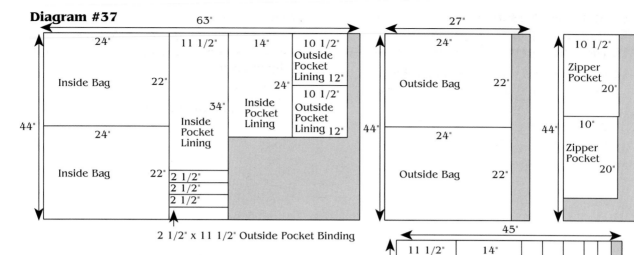

2 1/2" x 11 1/2" Outside Pocket Binding

3. Outside Pocket Bindings

- fold each of the 2 1/2" x 11 1/2" binding pieces in half lengthwise, WRONG SIDES TOGETHER and press.
- stitch a binding piece to the RIGHT SIDE top edge of both pockets, raw edges even.
- fold the binding pieces over the raw edges and pin to the WRONG SIDE of the pocket.
- stitch "in the ditch" along the right side of the binding making sure to catch the binding on the wrong side in the seam.
- stitch a binding piece to the right side lower edge of both pockets, raw edges even.
- do NOT press over.

4. Straps

- cut 1 strap in 1/2 to form two 4 1/2" x 22" pieces.
- stitch one short strap to one long strap 2 times.
- fold under 1/4" to the WRONG SIDE on one long side of each strap.
- lay the 2" x 66" pieces of batting on the WRONG SIDE of each strap.
- fold the long raw edge to the center of the batting.
- fold the long pressed edge to the center to cover the raw edge and pin.
- stitch through all layers along the edge of the pressed edge.

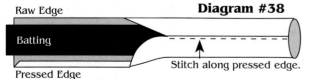

Diagram #38

Raw Edge

Batting

Pressed Edge

Stitch along pressed edge.

5. Apply Outside Pockets to Outside Bag

- center the outside pockets on the outside bags 3" above the lower raw edge.

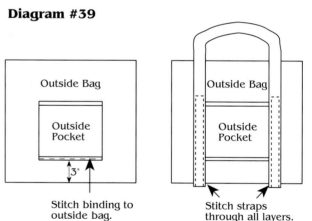

Diagram #39

Outside Bag

Outside Pocket

3"

Stitch binding to outside bag.

Outside Bag

Outside Pocket

Stitch straps through all layers.

- edge stitch the pressed edge of the binding to the outside bag.
- lay the strap, seam side down, on the outside bag. Begin about 1/2" past the lower edge, and up along each side of the outside pocket. Pin in place.
- stitch a rectangle on each strap as indicated on the diagram. The top of the rectangle stitching will be about 1" above the top edge of the outside pocket.

6. Complete the Outside Bag

- lay the two outside bags RIGHT SIDES TOGETHER matching raw edges and pin.
- stitch down one side edge, along the bottom edge and up the other side edge.
- open the bag at the bottom sewn edge and place the side seam even with the bottom seam, RIGHT SIDES TOGETHER.
- square the bottom of the bag by stitching across the corner.

Diagram #40

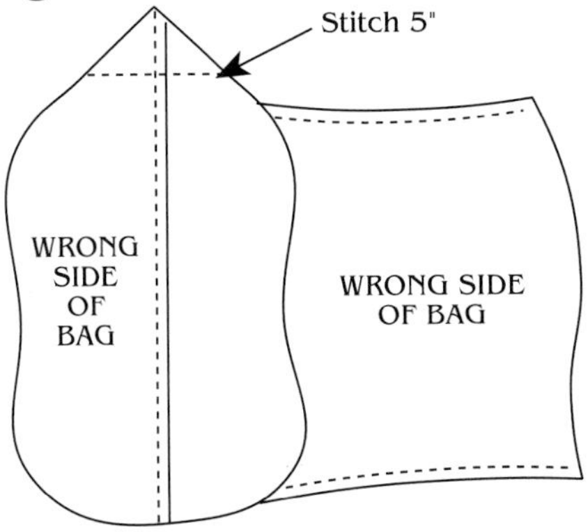

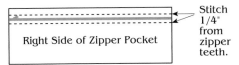

Stitch 5"

WRONG SIDE OF BAG

WRONG SIDE OF BAG

- repeat for the other corner of the bag.
- turn the bag to the right side.

7. Inside Pocket With Attached Zippered Pocket

Zippered Pocket

- cut the 10 1/2" x 20" zipper pocket into 2 pieces:
  1 – 8 1/2" x 20"
  1 – 2" x 20"
- fold under 1/4" on one 20" side of both pieces and press.
- lay the folded edges of the pocket piece wrong sides to the zipper.
- stitch 1/4" from the zipper teeth on both sides.

Diagram #41

Stitch 1/4" from zipper teeth.

Right Side of Zipper Pocket

- lay the 10 1/2" x 20" piece RIGHT SIDES TOGETHER over the zipper pocket and pin all raw edges together.
- stitch all around, clip corners and turn right sides out through the zippered opening. Press.
- center the zippered pocket on the right side of the 14" x 24" main pocket piece.
- edge stitch the zippered pocket to the main pocket piece.

Main Pocket

- lay the 14" x 24" inside pocket piece RIGHT SIDES TOGETHER with the 14" x 24" lining piece.
- stitch along the top 24" long edge.
- fold the pieces over so they are WRONG SIDES TOGETHER and press the top seam.
- fold 1/4" of the top edge of the pocket to the right side of the pocket and press. Edge stitch to form a self binding.
- lay the raw edges of the finished pocket RIGHT SIDES TOGETHER with the 1st inside bag 3" above the lower edge of the inside bag. See Diagram 42.

Diagram #42

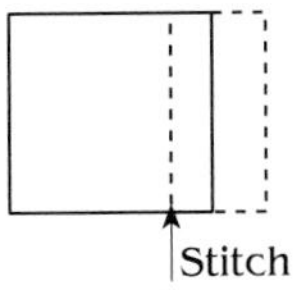

Stitch

- fold the pocket up onto the inside bag.
- sew a 2" piece of velcro to the inside of the pocket and to the inside bag.
- stitch all layers together at the sides to secure the pocket.

8. Second Inside Pocket

- lay the 11 1/2" x 34" inside pocket piece RIGHT SIDES TOGETHER with the 11 1/2" x 34" inside pocket lining.
- stitch along one 34" long edge.
- fold the pieces over so they are WRONG SIDES TOGETHER and press the top seam.
- fold 1/4" of the top edge of the pocket to the right side of the pocket and press. Edge stitch to form a self binding.
- mark the following measurements on the long raw edges of the pocket:

Diagram #43

Top edge folded over.

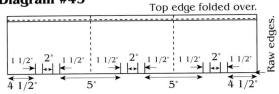

Raw edges.

1 1/2" | 2" | 1 1/2" | 1 1/2" | 2" | 1 1/2" | 1 1/2" | 2" | 1 1/2"

4 1/2" | 5" | 5" | 4 1/2"

- make 6 - 3/4" pleats at the 1 1/2" marking and pin.
- lay these raw edges of the second pocket RIGHT SIDES TOGETHER with the 2nd inside bag, 3" above the lower edge of the inside bag. See Diagram #42.
- fold the pocket up onto the inside bag.
- sew 3 - 2" pieces of velcro to the inside of the pocket placing them in the center of the three pleats of the pocket. See Diagram #43.

- mark 2 stitching lines on the pocket at the center point of the 5" spaces between the pleats. See Diagram #43.
- sew 3 - 2" pieces of the velcro to a position on the inside bag to align with the 3 pieces on the pocket.
- stitch all layers together at the sides to secure the pocket.
- stitch on the 2 marked lines through all layers to form 3 pockets.

9. Complete the Inside Bag

- lay the two inside bags RIGHT SIDES TOGETHER matching raw edges and stitch along the bottom edge.
- open the bag out and press the seam.
- lay the inside bag WRONG SIDES down on the 24" x 44" piece of batting.
- pin the raw edges of the inside bag to the batting.
- stitch close to the edge of all layers around the four edges.
- fold the inside bag RIGHT SIDES

TOGETHER in half and stitch both sides of the inside bag.
- square the bottom of the inside bag in the same manner as the outside bag.

10. Completing the Bag

- place the inside bag into the outside bag WRONG SIDES TOGETHER.
- line up the raw edges of the top of the bag, matching side seams and pin.
- sew the 2 – 2 1/2" x 44" pieces of top binding fabric together end for end.
- press this long strip in half lengthwise WRONG SIDES TOGETHER.
- beginning 1" from a side seam, fold 1/2" of the binding back on itself and pin to the right side of the bag, raw edges even.
- stitch the binding around the top of the bag overlapping the end of the binding over the folded beginning edge. Cut the extra binding off.
- fold the binding to the inside of the bag and hand stitch in place.

SECTION FOUR: The Five "E's"

You have now discovered as you've read and worked your way through the instructions and projects in the previous sections, how versatile this innovative grid system really is. The possibilities are endless and of course it is very difficult to contain them all in one book. This last Section – The Five "E's" – is designed to stimulate your creativity and to pass along a few suggestions for additional projects that you may want to try.

A. EXAMINE

I'm sure, as you have worked on some of the projects, you have had ideas and inspirations on further applications of the technique. This is the first step in the process of designing a project using the techniques in the book and also discovering a new application of the design. Examine the instructions, charts and diagrams throughout the book to ensure that you have a good understanding of the concept. Then take this knowledge one step further and apply it to a new project.

B. EXPLORE AND EXPERIMENT

This is where the fun begins! Explore the possibilities and then experiment with them. You'll be surprised when you see how these versatile designs can be applied. In the paragraphs below, you will find suggestions for some additional applications and embellishments for the designs in "Sugar 'n Spice".

1. FABRICS

Choice of fabric can greatly change the desired theme of a project.

- Changing from a light background to a dark background or visa versa, dramatically alters the appearance you may wish to project.
- Solid fabrics tend to present boldness and clarity while printed fabrics may be more subtle and sublime.
- Try using beiges, rust, browns, blacks, turquoises and burgundies to create the look of the southwest.
- Primary colours and youthful prints can make the projects suitable for a youngster.
- Fabrics that depict reality such as jungle prints in the dinosaur quilt can change the project from a child's delight to a modern interpretation of a bygone age.
- Use decorator fabrics that will compliment and accessorize a particular room or use fabrics that are suitable for the purpose of the project or the personality of the recipient.

2. EMBELLISHMENTS

The addition of a simple change to the design is sometimes enough to take the project from "it's O.K." to "it's outstanding!"

Prairie Points

– Prairie points are squares of fabric that are folded in such a way that they create a triangle with finished edges that can be used in place of a triangle on the design. See Diagram #45 for the method used to fold the square.

Diagram #45

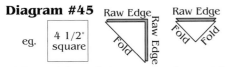

– This prairie point can now be used over a rectangle or square in a design to create a 3-D effect. See Diagram #46.

Diagram #46

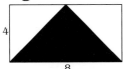

– one component from a design
– 4 grids x 8 grids
– using a 1/2" finished grid the rectangle would be cut 2 1/2" x 4 1/2"

– Normally with the grid system, the rectangle would be cut from the black fabric and the corner triangles would be cut from the white fabric.

– To make a prairie point, cut the rectangle from the white fabric. Cut a 4 1/2" square from the black fabric and fold it into a prairie point. Lay the raw edges of the prairie point along one 4 1/2" raw edge of the rectangle.

– Treat this unit the same as the sewn unit you would have made for the original design.

Diagram #47

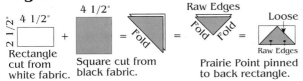

– These prairie points work exceptionally well for the humps on the dinosaurs and on the border of the Brontosaurus Joe. Try them for the ears on the kittens, the bows on the dolls hair or use them in an application of your own design.

Embellishment Additions

– Braid, ric rac, lace or ribbon will work wonderfully to add that special "Spice" to your project. Lay the embellishment over or between the edges of a triangle before it is sewn into the project or complete the

project and then apply the embellishment. The method you use will depend on the look you wish to achieve.

– You may wish to replace a narrow border with a ribbon or add a ribbon to a fabric border.

– **Kittens:** make the neck on the kittens without a bow in the piecework and then make a ribbon or a fabric bow and hand stitch it to the neck. This will achieve a truly dimensional look.

– Buttons could be used for the eyes on the kittens or to create eyes on the dinosaurs and dolls. The accent piece on the dolls dress could be embellished by the use of buttons.

– The use of lamé in your piecework can create a sophistication and special presence to your project. Apply an iron-on interfacing to the lamé and you then may use it in your projects as easily as the other cottons.

– The poems in the book may apply personally to the recipient of your project and you may want to incorporate these into your designs. Hand or machine embroider the poems onto the open space on the project or you may wish to apply the poem to a separate piece of fabric and stitch this to the backing of the quilt.

3. DESIGN CHANGES AND ADDITIONS

Doll Pocket Wall Hanging
(Cats and Dinosaurs may also be used.)

– make 4 doll blocks using the same method as for making the bibs, soft sculpture, pillow and tote.

– use the 1/2" finished grid for the blocks.

– the blocks should be 7 1/2" wide x 8 1/2" high, raw edge to raw edge when completed.

– cut lining fabric for each block the same size as the block.

– lay the lining piece RIGHT SIDE TOGETHER with the block and stitch the top edges.

– turn the block right side out and press the seam.

– cut 2 pieces of contrasting fabric 7 1/2" wide x 42 1/2" long.

– cut a piece of thermolam the same size.

– layer the thermolam between the WRONG SIDES of the two contrasting fabric pieces and pin well to hold in place.

– evenly space the doll blocks on the contrasting fabric, mark and stitch each block RIGHT SIDES TOGETHER with the contrasting fabric along the bottom edge of the block through all layers. Fold the block up onto the contrasting fabric and pin the blocks to the layered base along both side edges.

Diagram #48

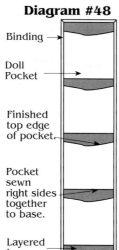

- make straight strip binding and apply to the four raw edges of the wall hanging as shown on Page 15 and 16.

- this pocket wall hanging could easily be adapted to incorporate the dinosaur or kitten blocks.

Kittens in a Square

- here is an easy adaptation to the kittens that would make a wonderful wall hanging or quilt.

Diagram #49

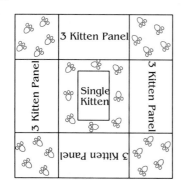

Quilt or Wall Hanging sizes before borders will be:

1/4" Finished Grid	13 1/2" x 13 1/2"
1/2" Finished Grid	27" x 27"
3/4" Finished Grid	40 1/2" x 40 1/2"
1" Finished Grid	54" x 54"
1 1/4" Finished Grid	67 1/2" x 67 1/2"
1 1/2" Finished Grid	71" x 71"

Zippered Baby Blankets

- the Brontosaurus Joe wall hanging and the Rows 'n Bows wall hanging work perfectly to make these zippered baby bunting blankets.

- sew the designs as shown in the instructions.

- stitch a zipper half to both short edges of the pieced top. See Diagram #50.

- you may wish to use a batting with a higher loft than you would with a wall hanging.

- cut the backing and batting slightly larger than the pieced front.

- layer the pieced front RIGHT SIDES

Diagram #50

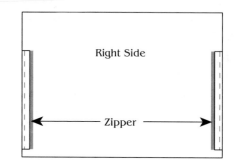

TOGETHER with the backing and place the batting on the WRONG SIDE of the backing. See Diagram #51.

Diagram #51

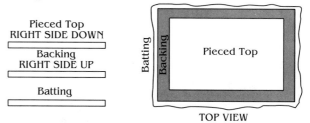

TOP VIEW

- stitch through all layers using the raw edge of the pieced top as the seam guide.

- leave a 3" - 4" opening along the bottom edge for turning, turn the quilt right sides out through the opening.

- hand stitch the opening closed.

- apply snaps or velcro as shown in the diagram to create a bunting bag.

Diagram #52

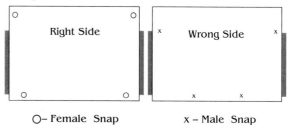

O – Female Snap   x – Male Snap

Soft Sculpture Toys

- turn the soft sculptures into soft toys by stuffing the sewn unit to form a more rounded, cuddly toy.

Notebook or Photo Album Cover

- use the designs for the bib, soft sculpture, pillow and tote to create a unique cover for a notebook or photo album. What a special gift this would make!

Clothing

- the single designs of the doll, dinosaur or kitten make wonderful additions to T-shirts, jackets, vests, nighties or pajamas.

– make sure the blocks are either applied directly to the clothing or lined to prevent ravelling of the raw edges of the pieced block.

4. BACK ART

If you want to take your quilted project one step further into the exciting realm of design variation, try using some back art for your backing instead of the usual one colour backing.

Dino-Mite!

– The back art on this quilt can be seen on the inset of the picture of the Dino-Mite quilt shown on Page 33.

– The back art uses blocks of the fabrics used on the front of the quilt as well as alphabet blocks spelling the words Dino-Mite. See Diagram #53 for the arrangement of the blocks.

Diagram #53

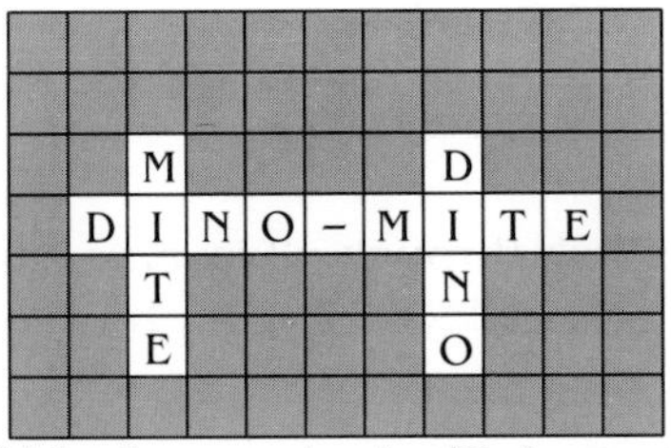

Back Art for Dino-Mite!

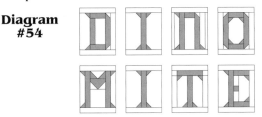

– The number of blocks required will depend on the size of your quilt.

– See Diagram #54 for the piecing designs for the alphabet blocks.

Diagram #54

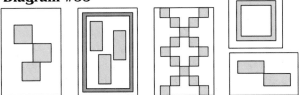

Navajo Friendship

– Put 3 cacti into the main backing fabric on the Navajo Friendship Quilt. This is a novel method to relate the back art of the quilt to the quilt top.

Diagram #55

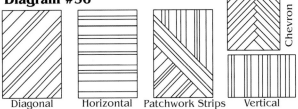

– When you are piecing the blocks for the front of the quilt project, make some extras at the same time and you can use these for your back art. Try to make the blocks for the back of the quilt fairly large so that fewer are needed to piece the back. Diagram #55 shows some possible arrangements of blocks for the back art.

– Try piecing the back art with strips of fabric leftover from the front. See Diagram #56 for suggestions.

Diagram #56

Diagonal   Horizontal   Patchwork Strips   Vertical   Chevron

– If you decide to try some back art, purchase more than required of each of the fabrics that you will be using for the quilt front. How much more of each fabric will depend on how many fabrics and how large the quilt will be. Figure out approximately how much fabric would be needed for a one fabric backing and divide this by the number of fabrics you will be using. Eg. 6 yards of fabric divided by 8 fabrics = 3/4 yard. I would recommend purchasing slightly more than this of each fabric to allow for piecing.

NOTE: Don't worry if you run out of fabric for the back art! Substitute a fabric of similar colour and value and space this evenly throughout your back art.

C. EXCITEMENT

Throughout the entire process of quilt-making from the initial steps of design to the choosing of the fabrics, to the piecework and finally to the last step of binding application, something flows through all of us. It is a feeling of excitement that non-quilters do not truly understand as they have not experienced the highs and lows of the quiltmaking process. As each project progresses, excitement builds with the completion of each component of the work. This feeling is what brings us back to the sewing room time after time even when we have no particular purpose for the project but merely wish to satiate the creative feeling that continues to build within us!

D. ELATION

The reason we do it all! The decisions have been made, the cutting and piecework completed, the layering, pinning and quilting is finished and finally the binding sewn on. The project is complete! Whether you are admiring your work yourself or the recipient of the project is happily enjoying the gift, the same feeling of elation is there. A job well done – what could be more satisfying! Well ... maybe the next one!

SECTION FIVE: Diagrams

A. Doll-ightful Quilt Options

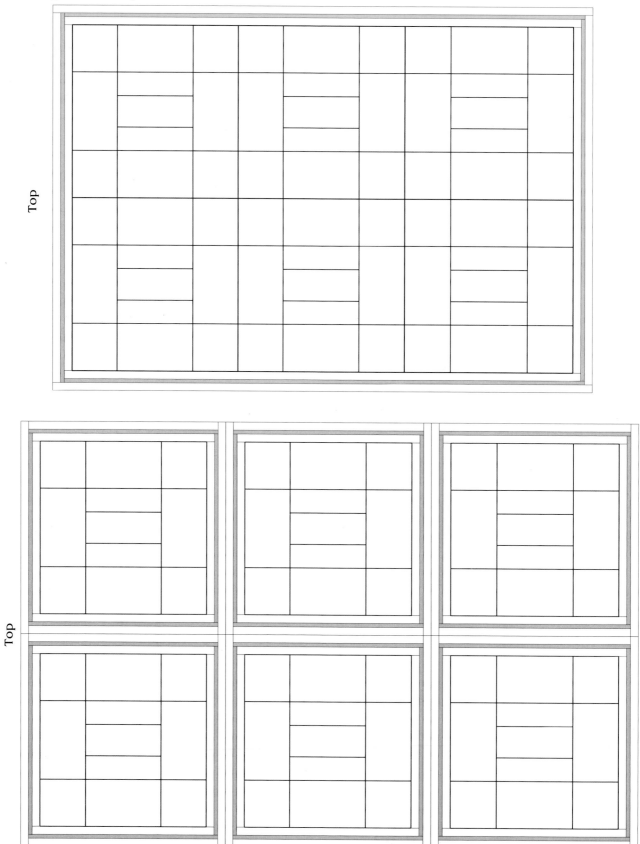

GRID for
Sugar & Spice & Other Things Nice

GRID for
Sugar & Spice & Other Things Nice

GRID for
Sugar & Spice & Other Things Nice

CUT ✂